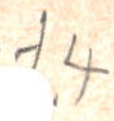

HIPPO B

# Roc
# Missiles

by John W. R. Taylor

completely revised and updated

HAMLYN
LONDON · NEW YORK · SYDNEY · TORONTO

## AS.30 (France)

Air-to-surface guided missile

*Built by:* Société Nationale Industrielle Aérospatiale

### CONFIGURATION

Bullet-shape body, with four fixed swept-back wings, which are canted to spin-stabilise missile in flight. Four 'flip-out' tail-fins indexed in line with wings. There are no control surfaces. Instead, the missile is steered by deflecting the exhaust gases from the sustainer motor.

### ENGINE

Dual-thrust solid-propellent rocket motor.

### GUIDANCE

Radio command type. The operator in the launch aircraft has a small control stick, by which he steers the missile to the target. Alternatively the AS.30 can use a Nord semi-automatic tracking system. With this, the operator keeps an optical sight aimed on the target, and the missile is held on course automatically by infra-red guidance.

### WARHEAD

High-explosive charge, weighing 510 lb. and fitted with alternative delay or non-delay fuse.

### DIMENSIONS

*Length:* 12′ 9½″. *Wing span:* 3′ 3½″.
*Body diameter:* 1′ 1½″.

### WEIGHT

1,146 lb.

### PERFORMANCE

*Range:* 7½ miles.

**The AS.30 is a larger version of the earlier, very successful AS.20* and the two missiles are shown side-by-side under the wings of a Vautour twin-jet fighter in the picture opposite. It is carried by the Dassault Mirage III–E supersonic fighters of the French Air Force and Dassault Etendard IV–M fighters of the French Navy. The R.A.F. bought at least 1,000 to equip its ground-attack Canberras and the AS.30 has also been supplied to the West German, South African and Swiss Air Forces.**

* *The AS.*20 *is* 8′ 6½″ *long, weighs* 315 *lb., has a* 66 *lb. warhead and a range of* 4½ *miles.*

N10
946

# ASROC (RUR–5A) (U.S.A.)

Rocket-boosted anti-submarine weapon

*Built by:* Honeywell Inc.

## CONFIGURATION

The airframe of Asroc consists simply of a short aluminium cylinder, made in two halves which are hinged to open like the jaws of an alligator, and fitted with four fixed fins. It connects the rocket motor at the rear to the payload at the front.

## ENGINE

One Naval Propellant Plant solid-propellent rocket motor.

## GUIDANCE

None in flight.

## WARHEAD

Payload can be either a General Electric Mk. 44 or Honeywell Mk. 46 high-speed acoustic homing torpedo or a nuclear depth charge, weighing about 500 lb.

## DIMENSIONS

*Length:* 15′. *Fin span:* 2′ 6″.
*Body diameter:* 1′.

## WEIGHT

1,000 lb.

## PERFORMANCE

Secret. Range believed to be from 1 to 6 miles.

**The Asroc (anti-submarine rocket) equips U.S. destroyers, escort vessels and cruisers. Within seconds of a submarine being detected by sonar, a fire-control computer in the ship works out the submarine's course, range and speed. The missile launcher (left picture) swings to face the target and the ship's commander fires one or more of the eight missiles, choosing the type of warhead best suited for the particular attack. The missile is aimed very accurately by the computer and follows a ballistic trajectory to the target. On receipt of a signal from the ship, it sheds its motor and airframe. If the payload is a torpedo, this is lowered by parachute into the water and then homes on to the submarine. The Asroc depth charge sinks to a predetermined depth and detonates with sufficient force to sink any submarine within a large radius. Asroc is also carried on Terrier missile launchers.**

# BLOODHOUND (Great Britain)

Surface-to-air guided missile

*Built by:* British Aircraft Corporation (Guided Weapons) Ltd.

## CONFIGURATION

Basic missile has an aeroplane layout with a bullet-shape fuselage, pivoting wings and a fixed tailplane. The engines are mounted above and below the body. The solid-propellent boosters are attached in pairs on each side of the body, and are each fitted with a large stabilising fin.

## ENGINES

Two Rolls-Royce Bristol Thor ramjet sustainers. Four jettisonable solid-propellent rocket boosters which drop away when burned out.

## GUIDANCE

Semi-active homing type. Ferranti Firelight or AEI Scorpion target-illuminating radar used with Mk. 2.

## WARHEAD

High-explosive type, with proximity fuse.

## DIMENSIONS

*Length:* 27′ 9″ with boosters, 25′ 2″ without boosters.
*Wing span:* 9′ 3½″. *Body diameter:* 1′ 9½″.

## WEIGHT AND PERFORMANCE

Secret, but range more than 50 miles.

**Bloodhound is the R.A.F.'s standard anti-aircraft missile and several squadrons are operational in the United Kingdom and overseas. The original Bloodhound Mk. 1 has been superseded by the improved Mk. 2 in the R.A.F. and Mk 2's are also used by the defence forces of Sweden, Switzerland and Singapore.**

**Bloodhound uses a ground-based radar to 'illuminate' the target and produce the reflected signals on which the missile homes. The Mk. 2 has much-improved CW (continuous-wave) radar guidance, which is less easy to jam and enables the Bloodhound to destroy high-speed aircraft at heights below 1,000 ft., which is too low for many large missiles. The Mk. 2 also has more powerful ramjets, greater range and greater destructive power. It is steered entirely by its wings, which can pivot together or differentially.**

# BOMARC (CIM–10B) (U.S.A.)

Long-range surface-to-air guided missile

*Built by:* The Boeing Company

## CONFIGURATION

Bomarc is a true pilotless fighter-plane, with an aeroplane layout. The tip of the tail-fin, almost all of the tailplane and the outer sections of the wings are pivoted to act as control surfaces. The two ramjet sustainers are carried on pylons under the body.

## ENGINES

Two 12,000-lb. s.t. Marquardt RJ43–MA–7 ramjets, running on kerosene. To propel the missile to a high enough speed for the ramjets to work efficiently, there is a 50,000-lb.s.t. Thiokol M51 solid-propellent booster rocket in the tail.

## GUIDANCE

Western Electronics radio command guidance for cruising flight. Westinghouse active homing system for final interception.

## WARHEAD

Nuclear type.

## DIMENSIONS

*Length:* 45′ 1″.
*Wing span:* 18′ 2″.
*Body diameter:* 2′ 11″

## WEIGHT

16,032 lb.

## PERFORMANCE

*Range:* 440 miles.
*Speed:* 1,850 m.p.h.

**Bomarc was the first long-range surface-to-air missile in service. The original CIM–10A version had a range of 250 miles and became operational at five U.S. bases, each of which had one or two 28-missile squadrons. It has been replaced by the improved CIM–10B, which equips six U.S. and two Canadian bases. Bomarcs are stored horizontally in firing shelters and can be erected and launched in a few seconds. Firing and guidance in flight are performed semi-automatically by North America's electronic defence system.**

# BULLPUP (AGM–12) (U.S.A.)

Air-to-surface guided missile

*Built by:* Martin Marietta Corporation and Maxson Electronics Corporation

## CONFIGURATION

Cylindrical body with pointed nose-cone. Four fixed wings at rear. Four small control surfaces on nose.

## ENGINE (AGM–12B)

One 12,000 lb s.t. Thiokol LR58–2 pre-packaged liquid-propellent rocket motor. No booster.

## GUIDANCE

Radio command system. Pilot steers missile to target by means of a small hand-switch.

## WARHEAD

High-explosive in all versions except AGM–12D which can have alternative nuclear warhead.

## DIMENSIONS (AGM–12B)

*Length:* 10′ 6″. *Wing span:* 3′ 1″.
*Body diameter:* 1′.

## WEIGHT (AGM–12B)

571 lb.

## PERFORMANCE (AGM–12B)

*Range:* 7 miles. *Speed:* 1,200 m.p.h.

**The original AGM–12A Bullpup of 1959 was a very simple solid-propellent missile built around a standard 250-lb. bomb. It has been followed by the AGM–12B Bullpup A with improved warhead and a liquid-propellent ' pre-packaged ' motor which can be stored for long periods in a fully fuelled condition. Bullpup A is used by the U.S. Navy and U.S.A.F. as a ground attack and anti-shipping weapon, and has been built under licence in Europe for NATO air forces. Also in service are the larger (13 ft. 7 in. long), longer-range (10 miles) AGM–12C Bullpup B, with heavier high-explosive warhead, for the U.S. Navy, and the AGM–12D with alternative nuclear warhead for the U.S.A.F. These weapons equip most of America's current attack aircraft, including the Phantom II, Thunderchief, Vigilante, Crusader and Intruder. AGM–12B Bullpups also arm the Royal Navy's Buccaneers. The illustration opposite shows AGM–12B Bull-pups on a U.S. Navy attack aircraft.**

NAVY

# FALCON (AIM–4A, C, D and H), SUPER FALCON (AIM–4F and G) and NUCLEAR FALCON (AIM–26A and B) (U.S.A.)

Air-to-air guided missiles
*Built by:* Hughes Aircraft Co.

*Illustrated opposite, left to right:* AIM–26A, AIM–4A, AIM–4C, AIM–4F

**CONFIGURATION**
Falcon has a cylindrical body and four long-chord delta wings, with a control surface to the rear of each wing. It has four small fins immediately aft of its rounded nose. Super Falcon is similar, but has a pointed nose-cone, bigger wings and no nose-fins. Nuclear Falcon has a rounded nose and bulged body.

**ENGINE**
All versions have a Thiokol solid-propellent rocket motor. That in the Falcon is a 6,000-lb.s.t. M58–E4.

**GUIDANCE**
The AIM–4A Falcon, AIM–4F Super Falcon and AIM–26A and B Nuclear Falcon all have a Hughes semi-active radar homing system. The AIM–4C, D and H Falcon and AIM–4G Super Falcon have an infra-red homing device behind glass noses. The AIM–4H is a modified D with laser proximity fuse for close-range combat.

**WARHEAD**
All versions have a high-explosive warhead except the AIM–26A which has a small nuclear warhead.

**DIMENSIONS**
*Length:* AIM–4A 6′ 6″, AIM–4C 6′ 7½″, AIM–4F 7′ 2″, AIM–4G 6′ 9″, AIM–26A 7′.
*Wing span:* AIM–4A and C 1′ 8″, AIM–4F and G 2′, AIM–26A 1′ 8″.
*Body diameter:* AIM–4A and C 6.4″, AIM–4F and G 6.6″, AIM–26A 11″.

**WEIGHT**
AIM–4A 110 lb., AIM–4C 122 lb., AIM–4F 150 lb., AIM–4G 145 lb., AIM–26A 203 lb.

**PERFORMANCE**
*Range:* AIM–4A and C, and AIM–26A 5 miles, AIM–4F and G 7 miles.
*Speed:* AIM–4A and C, and AIM–26A 1,400 m.p.h., AIM–4F and G 1,650 m.p.h.

**Since the Falcon entered production in 1954, Hughes have built about 25,500 AIM–4A's and C's and several thousand of the later models. Falcons are standard armament on the F–101B Voodoo, F–102 Delta Dagger and F–4 Phantom II. Super Falcons are carried by the F–106 Delta Dart and Nuclear Falcons by the Delta Dagger.**

U.S. AIR FORCE

## FIRESTREAK (Great Britain)

Air-to-air guided missile

*Built by:* Hawker Siddeley Dynamics Ltd.

### CONFIGURATION

Cylindrical body. Pointed nose, made up of eight flat glass panels, covering the infra-red guidance unit. Four fixed wings, well back on body. Four small tail control surfaces, indexed in line with wings. Two narrow bands of windows for infra-red proximity fuse around front of missile.

### ENGINE

Solid-propellent rocket motor.

### GUIDANCE

Infra-red homing.

### WARHEAD

High-explosive type, wrapped around the motor and weighing about 50 lb. Detonated by proximity fuse.

### DIMENSIONS

*Length:* 10′ 5$\frac{1}{2}$″. *Wing span:* 2′ 5$\frac{1}{2}$″.
*Body diameter:* 8$\frac{3}{4}$″.

### WEIGHT

300 lb.

### PERFORMANCE (approx)

*Range:* 0.75 to 5 miles.
*Speed:* over 1,400 m.p.h.

**Development of this highly efficient missi began in 1951 and it has been standard arm ment on R.A.F. and Royal Navy fighters fc many years. Two can be carried by th Lightning, four by the Sea Vixen. Like a infra-red missiles, the guidance equipme picks up the heat from the exhaust of a enemy aircraft and ' locks on ' to it. Whe the missile is fired, it homes on the hea source. One drawback with Firestreak is tha it can be fired only from behind the targe This has been overcome in the improved Re Top missile (see page 70).**

**The illustration opposite shows the twin Firestreak missile pack of a Lightning.**

# ‘ FROG–1 ’ (Russia)

Surface-to-surface unguided rocket

## CONFIGURATION

Slim cylindrical body, with a large warhead on the front and six fixed tail-fins. The current version, first seen in the 1960 May Day Parade through Moscow, has a parallel-sided warhead, as shown in the picture opposite.

## ENGINE

Solid-propellent rocket motor with seven nozzles. No booster.

## GUIDANCE

None. Missile is spin-stabilised in flight, like its American counterpart, Honest John.

## WARHEAD

Nuclear or thermo-nuclear types.

## DIMENSIONS (approx)

*Length:* 31′. *Fin span:* 3′ 3″.

## WEIGHT (estimated)

6,000 lb.

## PERFORMANCE (estimated)

*Range:* 15 miles.

**In service with the Soviet Army since at least 1957, this is the largest of a series of field artillery rockets known to NATO forces by the designation ‘ Frog ’, standing for ‘ Free Rocket Over Ground ’. Its body is always enclosed in a heavy ribbed casing, which contains guide-rails and may provide heating to keep the propellents warm and ready for action in low-temperature conditions. Photographs have shown that this casing is kept in position while the missile is elevated for firing.**

**The amphibious tracked transporter-launch vehicle which carries the ‘ Frog–1 ’ is also used with early versions of another artillery rocket known to NATO as ‘ Scud–A ’. This missile is about 35 ft. long and has a more conventional shape, with a pointed nose-cone of the same diameter as its body. It is believed to have a liquid-propellent engine and some form of guidance, giving increased accuracy over ranges up to about 50 miles. An improved ‘ Scud–B ’ was shown in a Moscow parade in November 1965, carried on a new wheeled transporter-erector-launch vehicle.**

# ‘ FROG–2, 3, 4, 5 and 7 ’ (Russia)

Surface-to-surface unguided rockets

## CONFIGURATION

The original ‘ Frog–2 ’, first seen in 1957, had a slim one-piece cylindrical body with four fixed tail-fins and with a bulbous warhead at the front, shaped like that of the American Honest John. ‘ Frog–3 ’ appeared to change to a tandem two-stage configuration with a more cylindrical warhead. It was followed by ‘ Frog–4 ’, which differs only in having a warhead of the same diameter as the body of the missile, and ‘ Frog–5 ’ with a further change of warhead. The latest ‘ Frog–7 ’ is a more compact weapon and has reverted to the original single-stage configuration.

## ENGINE

All versions appear to have solid-propellent rocket motors. The main first-stage nozzle is surrounded by a ring of smaller nozzles.

## GUIDANCE

None. Missile is almost certainly spin-stabilised in flight.

## WARHEAD

Probably interchangeable nuclear or high-explosive types.

## DIMENSIONS (‘ Frog–3 ’, approx)

*Length:* 33′ 6″. *Fin span:* 3′ 6″.

## WEIGHT (‘ Frog–3 ’, estimated)

4,400 lb.

## PERFORMANCE (‘ Frog–3 ’, estimated)

*Range:* 30 miles.

**Like ‘ Frog–1 ’, this family of unguided artillery rockets has been standard equipment in the Soviet Army for over 10 years. ‘ Frog–2, 3, 4 and 5 ’ are carried on a tracked vehicle derived from the PT76 amphibious reconnaissance tank, which serves also as the erector-launcher. The newer ‘ Frog–7 ’, first seen in November 1965, is transported on a wheeled type of erector-launch vehicle. The version illustrated opposite is ‘ Frog–5 ’.**

# ‘GANEF’ (Russia)

Mobile surface-to-air guided missile

## CONFIGURATION

Cylindrical main body, with a bullet-shape nose-cone mounted in the centre of the air intake at the front. Control surfaces consist of four pivoted wings on the forward part of the body. Four fixed tail-fins indexed at 45° to wings. Four solid-propellent boosters are ‘wrapped’ around the rear of the body.

## ENGINES

Ramjet sustainer integral with main body of missile. Four jettisonable solid-propellent boosters.

## GUIDANCE

Command guidance system.

## WARHEAD

Probably high-explosive type.

## DIMENSIONS (approx)

*Length:* 30′. *Wing span:* 7′ 6″. *Body diameter:* 2′ 8″.

## WEIGHT AND PERFORMANCE

Secret.

**First seen in the 1964 May Day parade through Moscow, this anti-aircraft missile, known to NATO by the code-name ‘Ganef’, is always carried in pairs on tracked vehicles and may also be intended for use in a surface-to-surface rôle. Its configuration, with the warhead forming a centre-body in an air intake at the front, implies the use of a ramjet sustainer engine. ‘Ganef’ is air-transportable, on its launch vehicle, in the Antonov An–22 heavy freight aircraft.**

# GENIE (AIR–2A) (U.S.A.)

Unguided air-to-air rocket

*Built by*: McDonnell Douglas Corporation

## CONFIGURATION

Cylindrical body, with larger-diameter warhead at the front and four tail-fins at the rear. Tips of fins are movable.

## ENGINE

Aerojet-General solid-propellent rocket motor of approx. 36,000 lb.s.t.

## GUIDANCE

None. Movable fin-tips are actuated by a gravity-correction device.

## WARHEAD

Nuclear warhead. This is not armed until a few moments before firing.

## DIMENSIONS

*Length:* 9′ 7″. *Fin span:* 2′.
*Body diameter:* 1′ 5½″.

## WEIGHT

820 lb.

## PERFORMANCE

*Range:* 6 miles. *Speed:* 2,000 m.p.h.

**Genie was the world's first air-to-air missile with a nuclear warhead. It was fired for the first time from an F–89 Scorpion fighter over Indian Springs, Nevada, on 19th July, 1957, at a height of about 15,000 ft. The pilot of the F–89 turned away sharply and the missile was detonated by a signal from the ground after travelling about three miles. U.S.A.F. observers stood under the point of the explosion for an hour afterwards, with no ill effects.**

**Genie is carried under the wings of the F–89, under the front fuselage of the F–101B Voodoo and inside the weapon-bay of the F–106 Delta Dart. It is normally fired automatically and detonated by the radar fire-control system of the launch aircraft, and has a lethal radius of at least 1,000 ft.**

1929

## ' GRIFFON ' (Russia)

Surface-to-air guided missile

### CONFIGURATION

Tandem two-stage layout. Cylindrical body with four fixed wings, mounted well back, and four small tail control surfaces indexed in line with wings. Small trailing-edge control surface inset in each wing-tip. Booster unit has four large fixed fins, indexed at 45° to wings.

### ENGINES

Solid-propellent booster. Not known whether sustainer is solid or liquid-propellent.

### GUIDANCE

Probably a similar radar command system to that used for ' Guideline '.

### WARHEAD

Probably interchangeable nuclear and high-explosive types.

### DIMENSIONS (approx)

*Length:* 54′. *Wing span:* 12′. *Body diameter:* 2′ 10″.

### WEIGHT AND PERFORMANCE

Secret.

**When this mighty missile was first included in a parade through Moscow, in November 1963, the commentator described it as an anti-missile missile. By this, he probably meant that it is capable of intercepting certain classes of tactical ballistic and air-launched missiles, rather than weapons like Polaris and Minuteman. ' Griffon ' appears to be a development of the ' Guideline ' type of weapon system, just as the American Spartan missile is being evolved from the Nike family. It almost certainly requires elaborate ground equipment and the vehicle on which it was displayed was no more than a transport trolley.**

# ‘GUIDELINE’ (SAM–2) (Russia)

Surface-to-air guided missile

## CONFIGURATION

Tandem two-stage layout. Cylindrical body with four fixed wings, mounted well back, and four small tail control surfaces indexed in line with wings. Four small vanes on nose. Booster unit has four large fixed fins, indexed in line with wings. Control surfaces are hinged to the trailing-edges of two of the booster fins.

## ENGINE

One liquid-propellent sustainer and a solid-propellent booster.

## GUIDANCE

Target is tracked by radar, which feeds signals to a computer, from which guidance signals are radioed to missile.

## WARHEAD

High-explosive type, weighing 288 lb.

## DIMENSIONS (approx.)

*Length:* 35′. *Wing span:* 5′ 7″.
*Body diameter:* 1′ 8″.

## WEIGHT

*With booster:* 4,875 lb.

## PERFORMANCE

*Range:* 28 miles. *Speed:* 2,200 m.p.h.
*Effective ceiling:* 60,000′.

**This anti-aircraft weapon has been seen regularly in Moscow military parades since 1957 and was probably the first surface-to-air guided missile to enter service in the Soviet Union. It is in much the same class as the U.S. Nike Ajax and has been supplied to Russia's friends and allies throughout the world, including Cuba, Egypt, Indonesia, Iraq and the Warsaw Pact countries of Europe. Many ‘Guidelines’ have been fired against U.S. aircraft over North Vietnam, with only limited success. However, by compelling American pilots to fly at low altitude, where ‘Guideline’ is not effective, they have enabled conventional anti-aircraft gunfire to take heavy toll of U.S. aircraft. The latest version, first seen in 1967, has a larger nose-cone, without vanes.**

# HAWK (MIM–23A) (U.S.A.)

Surface-to-air guided missile

*Built by:* Raytheon Co. and in Europe

## CONFIGURATION

Bullet-shape body, with four long-chord wings. Moveable control surface on trailing-edge of each wing.

## ENGINE

One Aerojet-General M22–E8 dual-thrust solid-propellent motor.

## GUIDANCE

Raytheon continuous-wave semi-active radar homing system.

## WARHEAD

Variety of high-explosive types.

## DIMENSIONS

*Length:* 16′ 6″. *Wing span:* 3′ 11½″. *Body diameter:* 1′ 2″.

## WEIGHT

1,295 lb.

## PERFORMANCE

*Range:* 22 miles. *Speed:* 1,600 m.p.h.

**Hawk (Homing All-the-Way Killer) was developed for the U.S. Army to provide defence against low-flying aircraft. It has proved its effectiveness in firings against target aircraft at all altitudes from tree-top level to about 40,000 ft. and can sort out moving target at low altitudes from a mass of signals reflected by trees, buildings and hills. It became the first missile to destroy ballistic rocket when it intercepted an Honest John over White Sands Missile Range in January 1960, and later brought down smaller Littlejohn and a Corporal. The U.S. Army and Marine Corps have Hawk battalions, each with 6–12 triple launchers, in Germany, Vietnam, Korea, the Panama Canal Zone and Okinawa. Hawk has also been built by Mitsubishi in Japan and by a group of companies in France, West Germany, Italy, Belgium and the Netherlands for the armies of those countries, and has been supplied to Sweden, Israel, Spain, Taiwan and Saudi Arabia. The photo opposite shows a Hawk triple launcher and, in the foreground, the tracked vehicle used to reload launchers. Both of these units can be transported by standard U.S. assault aircraft and helicopters. Some American units have re-equipped with self-propelled tracked triple launch vehicles.**

# HONEST JOHN (MGR-1) (U.S.A.)

Unguided field artillery rocket

*Built by:* Douglas Aircraft Co., Inc., and The Emerson Electric Manufacturing Co.

## CONFIGURATION

Cylindrical body with large bulged warhead at front and four fixed tail-fins.

## ENGINE

One Hercules solid-propellent rocket motor. No booster.

## GUIDANCE

None. After launching, the missile is made to spin by a ring of small Thiokol rockets aft of the warhead. The tail-fins are canted to keep it spinning throughout its flight, so that it does not wander off course.

## WARHEAD

Variety of nuclear or high-explosive types, weighing about 1,500 lb.

## DIMENSIONS

*Length:* MGR-1A 27′ 3″, MGR-1B 24′ $9\frac{1}{2}$″.
*Body diameter:* 2′ 6″.
*Fin span:* MGR-1A 9′ 1″, MGR-1B 4′ 6″

## WEIGHT

MGR-1A 5,820 lb., MGR-1B 4,719 lb.

## PERFORMANCE

*Range:* 5–23 miles. *Speed:* 1,150 m.p.h

**During World War Two the Russians, th Western Allies and the Germans all use batteries of small rockets as highly mobil artillery. Honest John carried the process stage further by taking the place of heavy guns About 20,000 were produced for the Armies o America and its allies, including Britain, Italy France and Germany, and each can be fired b fewer than six men if necessary. Continue development produced the MGR-1B version which is smaller than the 'A' (as illustrate opposite) but has a higher performance. Als in service is the much smaller MGR- Littlejohn, which weighs only 780 lb. but ca carry a nuclear or high-explosive warhea about 10 miles.**

# HOUND DOG (AGM-28) (U.S.A.)

Air-to-surface stand-off bomb

*Built by:* North American Aviation, Inc.

## CONFIGURATION

Tail-first aeroplane layout, with slim cylindrical body and rear-mounted delta wings. Control is by means of the movable delta fore-planes, ailerons on the wing trailing-edges and a rudder hinged to the fixed vertical fin. The engine is carried on a pylon under the body.

## ENGINE

One 7,500-lb.s.t. Pratt & Whitney J52 turbojet. Kerosene fuel tanks in body.

## GUIDANCE

Autonetics inertial guidance system, supplemented by an automatic star-tracker which feeds information on the missile's position into the inertial system.

## WARHEAD

Thermonuclear (H-bomb) type.

## DIMENSIONS

*Length:* 42′ 6″. *Wing span:* 12′ 2″.
*Body diameter:* 2′ 4½″.

## WEIGHT

10,147 lb.

## PERFORMANCE

*Range:* over 600 miles.
*Speed:* 1,300 m.p.h.

**Hound Dog has been in service with B–52 Stratofortress squadrons of the U.S.A.F.'s Strategic Air Command since March 1960. Each of the B–52's carries two Hound Dogs on underwing pylons and the aircrews have found that they can shorten the bombers' take-off run by running the engines of the missiles to supplement the bombers' eight turbojets. This does not reduce the Hound Dogs' range as their fuel tanks can be topped up from the bombers' tanks during flight. Hound Dog can be programmed to deliver its final attack from high or low altitudes. The original AGM–28A version was superseded in 1961 by the improved AGM–28B, of which some 400 are available for combat use.**

# IKARA (Australia)

Long-range surface-to-underwater anti-submarine missile

*Built by:* Australian Government Aircraft Factories

## CONFIGURATION

The Ikara airframe consists of a body with short cropped-delta wings, elevon control surfaces and upper and lower vertical tail-fins. An acoustic homing torpedo is recessed into the bottom of the body.

## ENGINE

Dual-thrust solid-propellent rocket motor.

## GUIDANCE

Radio-radar command guidance, operated by prediction system on board launching ship.

## WARHEAD

American Type 44 acoustic homing torpedo.

## DIMENSIONS (approx)

*Length:* 11′. *Wing span:* 5′.

## WEIGHT AND PERFORMANCE

Secret.

**Initial development of this very effective anti-submarine weapon was carried out in Australia by the Department of Supply and Department of the Navy, for the Royal Australian Navy, with which Ikara has been in service for some time. A modified version, known as RN Ikara, is being developed for service with the Royal Navy.**

**Data from sonar detection equipment, carried by ships and helicopters, is fed to a computing system on board Ikara's launch-ship. Ikara is then ramp-launched in the direction of the target. A tracking and guidance system enables the torpedo to be separated and lowered into the water by parachute at the most favourable spot to ensure a ' kill '. Range of Ikara is said to be 20–50 nautical miles.**

# ‘KENNEL’ (Russia)

Air-to-surface stand-off bomb

## CONFIGURATION

‘Kennel’ is rather likc a miniature MiG–15 jet-fighter, with a tubby, circular-section fuselage and mid-set sweptback wings. Sweptback tail surfaces, with high-mounted tailplane. Conventional aeroplane-type control surfaces. Semi-circular air-intake in nose. No undercarriage. Radome on nose.

## ENGINE

Turbojet engine in fuselage.

## GUIDANCE

Probably by radio command from launching aircraft, but nose radome may contain some form of terminal homing system.

## WARHEAD

Unknown, but probably high-explosive.

## DIMENSIONS (approx)

*Length:* 28′. *Wing span:* 16′.

## WEIGHT AND PERFORMANCE

Secret, but range about 50 miles.

**Known as ‘Kennel’ to NATO forces, this little air-launched flying bomb has been in service with the Soviet Naval Air Force since about 1962. Two are carried on pylons under the wings of Tupolev Tu–16 twin-jet bombers, and are known to arm aircraft of this type supplied to the Indonesian and Egyptian air forces. Missiles very like ‘Kennel’, and known by the NATO code-name ‘Samlet’, are used in a surface-to-surface rôle, and have been supplied to Poland and Cuba, which have no bombers capable of carrying ‘Kennel’. Another development, in service with the Soviet Naval Air Force on Tu–16 bombers, is ‘Kelt’, a rocket-powered version of ‘Kennel’ with a probable range of 100 miles.**

# LANCE (XMGM–52A) (U.S.A.)

Surface-to-surface field artillery guided missile

*Built by:* Ling-Temco-Vought, Inc.

## CONFIGURATION

Cylindrical body, with ogival pointed nose-cone. Four small fixed tail-fins.

## ENGINE

One Rocketdyne pre-packaged liquid-propellent rocket engine.

## GUIDANCE

Simplified inertial system developed by U.S. Army Missile Command.

## WARHEAD

Interchangeable nuclear and high-explosive types.

## DIMENSIONS (approx)

*Length:* 20′. *Body diameter:* 1′ 10″.

## WEIGHT (approx)

3,200 lb.

## PERFORMANCE

*Minimum range:* 3 miles.
*Maximum range:* 30 miles.

**Known originally as Missile B, this highly mobile divisional support weapon has been under development by LTV since November 1962, to replace Honest John and possibly Littlejohn. Lance was fired for the first time in March 1965, achieving what has been described as the first-ever bulls-eye in an initial firing. Since then an extended-range version has been under development and this is to be the production model.**

**Lance can be deployed on either a self-propelled tracked launcher (SPL) or a fully mobile lightweight launcher (LWL). The LWL, complete with missile, can be carried by helicopter. The SPL with missile can be air-dropped from fixed-wing transport aircraft. A loader-transporter tracked vehicle carries two missiles and a hoist to reload the launcher.**

# MACE (CGM–13) (U.S.A.)

Surface-to-surface 'flying-bomb' missile

*Built by:* Martin Marietta Corporation

## CONFIGURATION

Aeroplane layout, with cigar-shape body, high-set sweptback wings and a T-tail. Engine air-intake in undersurface of body. CGM–13C has a large blister fairing under rear of body.

## ENGINE

One 5,200-lb.s.t. Allison J33–A–41 turbo-jet in rear of body. One 100,000-lb.s.t. Thiokol solid-propellent rocket booster is attached under tail for take-off and is jettisoned after burn-out.

## GUIDANCE

MGM–13B had Goodyear ATRAN (Automatic Terrain Recognition and Navigation) system, which compared data on a film strip with the terrain over which the missile flew and corrected immediately any deviation from course. CGM–13C has A.C. Spark Plug AChiever inertial guidance.

## WARHEAD

Nuclear type.

## DIMENSIONS

*Length:* 44′. *Wing span:* 22′ 11″. *Body diameter:* 4′ 6″.

## WEIGHT (CGM–13C)

approx. 18,000 lb.

## PERFORMANCE

*Range:* MGM–13B over 650 miles CGM–13C over 1,200 miles.
*Speed:* over 650 m.p.h.

**The Mace is a much improved development of the earlier Matador, with self-contained guidance systems which are immune to jamming. The MGM–13B was operational with the U.S.A.F.'s 38th Tactical Missile Wing in Europe for several years, until the mid-60's. The CGM–13C continues in first-line combat service in both Europe and Okinawa. Mace is carried with its wings folded, on a big articulated launch truck, with all its support equipment on a tractor train; but squadrons normally maintain their missiles, ready to fire, inside 'hardened' launch-shelters.**

# MALAFON (France)

Surface-to-surface or surface-to-underwater anti-submarine missile

*Built by:* Société Industrielle d'Aviation Latécoère

## CONFIGURATION

Aeroplane layout, with small pivoted mid-set wings well forward and high-set tailplane carrying twin fins. Tracking flare on each wing-tip. Torpedo housed in nose.

## ENGINE

No sustainer. Missile is launched by two solid-propellent booster rockets attached under body.

## GUIDANCE

Command system, operated by sonar in the ship from which the missile is launched.

## WARHEAD

21-in. acoustic homing torpedo, weighing 1,157 lb.

## DIMENSIONS

*Length:* 19′ 8″. *Wing span:* 9′ 10″.

## WEIGHT

2,865 lb.

## PERFORMANCE

*Range:* 11 miles. *Speed:* 515 m.p.h.

**This ingenious anti-submarine weapon is ramp launched from a ship by two booster rockets which accelerate it to 515 m.p.h. in 3 seconds. The boosters then fall away and the Malafon glides the rest of the way to the target. It is kept at a constant height of 330 ft. above the water by a radio-altimeter, which adjusts the incidence of the wings to provide increased lift as the missile's speed decreases. The ship's sonar keeps track of the submarine and guides the missile towards it. At a distance of about half a mile from the target, the missile is slowed by a tail parachute and the torpedo shoots forward out of the nose and into the water, where it homes on noise from the submarine. Thirteen ships of the French Navy are being equipped with Malafon.**

AFO
33
50

# MALKARA (Australia)

Vehicle-transported anti-tank guided missile

*Built by:* Australian Government Aircraft Factories

## CONFIGURATION

The steel and magnesium body has cylindrical front and rear sections, but is square in the centre, where the four pivoting wings (of foam-filled glass-cloth) are attached. The four fixed tail-fins are indexed at 45° to the wings.

## ENGINE

Dual-thrust solid-propellent rocket motor.

## GUIDANCE

Conventional wire guidance.

## WARHEAD

57·5-lb. high-explosive type.

## DIMENSIONS

*Length:* 6′ 5$\frac{1}{2}$″. *Wing span:* 2′ 7$\frac{1}{4}$″
*Body diameter:* 8″.

## WEIGHT

222 lb.

## PERFORMANCE

*Range:* 500 to 4,000 yards.
*Speed:* 327 m.p.h.

**More than twice as heavy as any anti-tan missile previously put into service, Malkar was designed to knock out even the heavies tank with one shot. It can be carried b armoured vehicles or small launch-cars of th type illustrated. Specially developed for th British Army, this vehicle can be dropped b parachute from aircraft like the R.A.F.' Argosy transport and can carry four Malkaras**

**In firing tests, Malkara demonstrated tha it can be used equally successfully agains enemy strong-points and bridges. Its accurac is such that it can be guided through th openings in a concrete bunker or gun emplace ment from more than a mile away. It i standard equipment in the British Army.**

## MARTEL (France–Great Britain)

Air-to-surface guided missile
*Built by:* S.A. Engins Matra and Hawker Siddeley Dynamics Ltd.

### CONFIGURATION
Cylindrical body with either pointed ogival nose (AS.37) or hemispherical glass nose (AJ.168). Four fixed wings, well back on body. Four tail control surfaces, immediately aft of wings and indexed in line with them.

### ENGINE
Hotchkiss-Brandt and Aérospatiale solid-propellent rocket motors.

### GUIDANCE
British version (AJ.168) flies towards target automatically, but is guided on the last stage before impact by the weapon operator in the launch aircraft, using a joystick or similar control system. This guidance is made possible by TV equipment in the nose of the missile, which transmits a direct visual picture of the target for display on a high-brightness monitor screen in the cockpit. The French version (AS.37) does not have TV guidance and is intended for anti-radar missions, homing automatically on the emissions from the target.

### WARHEAD
High-explosive.

### DIMENSIONS (approx.)
*Length:* AS.37 13′ 1½″, AJ.168 12
*Wing span:* 3′ 8″. *Body diameter:* 1′ 3′

### WEIGHT AND PERFORMANCE
Secret.

**Matra and HSD have developed the Marte as one of the growing number of Anglo-Frenc joint projects in the aerospace field. Apar from the interchangeable heads, for TV guid ance or anti-radar missions, the two version of Martel are identical, with a range of ‘ ten of miles ’ and the ability to overcome attempt to jam their guidance systems. Evaluation o both versions was under way by 1969 production orders have been placed and th Martel will eventually arm a variety of air craft, including the Buccaneers and Nimrod operated by the R.A.F. and the Mirage III–E’s Jaguars and Atlantics of the French Air Forc and Navy.**

# MASURCA Mk. 2 (France)

Surface-to-air, ship-launched guided weapon

*Developed by*: The Naval Arsenal at Ruelle

## CONFIGURATION

Tandem two-stage missile. The missile itself has a cylindrical body with pointed ogival nose-cone, four short-span wings of very long chord and four pivoted tail control surfaces, indexed in line with the wings. The tandem booster is also cylindrical, of greater diameter, with four fixed stabilising fins indexed in line with the wings.

## ENGINES

Both stages are powered by a solid-propellent rocket motor.

## GUIDANCE

Masurca Mk. 2 Mod. 2 has a beam-riding guidance system, supplied by CFTH/CSF and TRT. The Mk. 2 Mod. 3 version has a self-homing system by the same manufacturers.

## WARHEAD

High-explosive type weighing 105 lb., with proximity fuse.

## DIMENSIONS

*Length:* with booster 28′ 2½″, without booster 17′ 4½″. *Wing span:* 2′ 6″. *Booster fin span:* 4′ 11″. *Body diameter:* 1′ 4″.

## WEIGHTS

Mod. 2 with booster 4,387 lb., without booster 1,852 lb.

Mod. 3 with booster 4,585 lb., without booster 2,050 lb.

## PERFORMANCE

*Range:* over 25 miles.

*Speed:* over 1,650 m.p.h.

**After several years of development, including a major design change in the Mk. 2 version, Masurca (MArine SUpersonique Ruelle Contre Avions) is now in service on the French Navy's new guided missile frigates 'Suffren' and 'Duquesne', each of which carries 48 missiles. It will also arm the cruiser 'Colbert'. Masurca is similar in configuration to the American Advanced Terrier, but has a different type of guidance system. The original Mod. 2 beam-riding version was being superseded by the Mod. 3, with self-homing guidance, in 1970.**

28
28
28

# MINUTEMAN (LGM–30) (U.S.A.)

Intercontinental ballistic missile

*Built by*: The Boeing Co.

**CONFIGURATION**
Three-stage missile. Minuteman I and II are made up of four cylindrical sections of progressively reduced diameter, joined together by tapered fairings. The three lower sections are booster stages, containing the rocket engines and propellents. The top stage is the re-entry vehicle, which alone travels all the way to the target and contains the warhead. In Minuteman III the three upper sections all have the same diameter, with an ogival nose-cone fairing.

**ENGINES (LGM–30B)**
All three booster stages have solid-propellent motors, each with four swivelling nozzles for control purposes. The first stage is produced by Thiokol and has a stainless steel case. The second stage is by Aerojet-General and has a titanium case. Stage three is manufactured by Hercules Inc. and has a glass-plastic case. (LGM–30F differs in having a single nozzle in its second stage.)

**GUIDANCE**
Autonetics inertial system.

**WARHEAD**
Thermonuclear (H-bomb) type, with multiple independently targeted re-entry vehicles on LGM–30G.

**DIMENSIONS**
*Length:* LGM–30B 55′ 11″, LGM–30F and G 59′ 10″.
*Maximum body diameter:* 6′.

**WEIGHT** LGM–30B 65,000 lb., LGM–30F 70,000 lb. LGM–30G 76,000 lb.

**PERFORMANCE**
*Range:* LGM–30B 6,300 miles, LGM–30F over 7,000 miles, LGM–30G over 8,000 miles.
*Speed:* 14,500 m.p.h.

**This solid-propellent missile is smaller and easier to handle than the big liquid-propellent ICBM's which preceded it. A total of 1,000 have been delivered and are now at instant readiness in below-ground ' silos '. There are three wings (500 missiles) of LGM–30B Minuteman I's. Three other wings (each 150 missiles) have the much improved LGM–30F Minuteman II, with another 50 of these missiles emplaced adjacent to Wing I. All missiles will eventually be converted to Minuteman II or LGM–30G Minuteman III standard.**

## NIKE HERCULES (MIM–14A) (U.S.A.)

Surface-to-air guided missile

*Built by*: Western Electric Co., Inc., and Douglas Aircraft Co., Inc.

### CONFIGURATION

Two-stage missile. Missile itself has tapering cylindrical body, with four rear-mounted fixed wings. Control is by means of four small pivoted fore-planes, indexed in line with wings. The cylindrical booster is fitted with three large stabilising fins.

### ENGINES

The sustainer engine in the missile is an Aerojet-General liquid-propellent rocket. The booster contains a Hercules solid-propellent rocket motor.

### GUIDANCE

Radar command system, produced by Western Electric.

### WARHEAD

High-explosive type, detonated by a signal from the ground when the missile is at its closest point to the target.

### DIMENSIONS

*Length:* with booster 34′, without booster 21′.

*Wing span:* 4′ 5″. *Body diameter:* 1′.

### DIMENSIONS

*Length:* with booster 41′ 6″, without booster 27′.

*Wing span:* 6′ 2″. *Body diameter:* 2′ 7½″.

### WEIGHT

With booster 10,400 lb., without booster 5,200 lb.

### PERFORMANCE

*Range:* 80 miles.

*Speed:* 2,400 m.p.h.

**The Nike Hercules began to enter service in 1958 and has supplemented or replaced Nike Ajax at launch sites in the United States, Europe, Japan, Formosa and Okinawa. Although far more efficient than Nike Ajax, it can utilise the same basic launching equipment. About 80 batteries are still in service. Although most are at permanent sites, Nike Hercules can be deployed on mobile launchers. Proof of its effectiveness was given in September 1960, when one Nike Hercules intercepted and destroyed another at an altitude of 100,000 ft. and 30 miles from the defending missile's launching point. Mitsubishi is still manufacturing the Nike Hercules for the Japan Defence Agency.**

# PERSHING (MGM-31A) (U.S.A.)

Surface-to-surface field artillery missile

*Built by:* Martin Marietta Corporation

## CONFIGURATION

Two-stage missile. Main body is cylindrical, with a long tapered nose. Control is by means of three movable tail-fins on the first stage, deflection of the first-stage rocket exhaust, and three large vanes at the rear of the second stage.

## ENGINES

First and second-stage solid-propellent rocket motors are produced by Thiokol.

## GUIDANCE

Inertial system by Bendix Eclipse-Pioneer Division.

## WARHEAD

Nuclear type.

## DIMENSIONS

*Length:* 34′ 6″. *Body diameter:* 3′ 4″.

## WEIGHT

10,000 lb.

## PERFORMANCE

*Range:* 115–460 miles.
*Speed:* over 3,000 m.p.h.

**Development of Pershing was started in 1958 to replace the U.S. Army's Redstone. By then, the Government order restricting U.S. Army missiles to a range of less than 250 miles had been cancelled. As a result, although Pershing is only about half the size and weight of Redstone, it has a considerably longer range. Being a solid-propellent missile, it is easier to transport and handle and can be prepared for firing more quickly. In the initial form, in which it entered service in 1962, the missile and its support and firing equipment were all transported on four M474 tracked vehicles. In the new Pershing 1A weapon system, shown in the picture opposite, rate of firing and reliability are improved by mounting the missile and its equipment on XM656 wheeled vehicles. There is no change in the missile itself.**

U.S. ARMY
US ARMY

# PHOENIX (AIM–54A) (U.S.A.)

Air-to-air guided missile

*Built by*: Hughes Aircraft Co.

## CONFIGURATION

Phoenix (on right of picture opposite) has a cylindrical body with ogival nose. Four long-chord wings well back on body, with four pivoting tail control surfaces immediately aft and indexed in line.

## ENGINE

Rocketdyne solid-propellent rocket motor.

## GUIDANCE

Hughes radar homing system. Control system in launch aircraft locks on to target and launches missile, which then takes over and intercepts target.

## WARHEAD

Type unknown.

## DIMENSIONS

*Length*: 13′. *Wing span*: 3′.
*Body diameter*: 1′ 3″.

## WEIGHT

838 lb.

## PERFORMANCE

Secret.

**Designed for the next generation of U.S. interceptor aircraft, the two big, fast and powerful missiles illustrated opposite have range and performance capabilities never before achieved in missile design. The Phoenix (*right*) will arm the U.S. Navy's Grumman F–14A carrier-based fighter; it differs from previous Hughes air-to-air missiles in having tail control surfaces instead of the usual wing trailing-edge surfaces. Flight tests of powered development rounds have been underway successfully since September 1966. The other missile (*left*) is the AIM–47A, designed for use with the U.S.A.F.'s Lockheed YF–12A Mach 3 interceptor. It has longer-chord wings than Phoenix, a Lockheed pre-packaged liquid-propellent engine and interchangeable nuclear and high-explosive warheads.**

# POLARIS (UGM–27) (U.S.A.)

Submarine-launched ballistic missile

*Built by:* Lockheed Missiles and Space Co.

## CONFIGURATION

The squat cylindrical body is made up of two solid-propellent rocket motors. In Polaris A2, it is joined to the slim cylindrical warhead by a tapered fairing. Polaris A3 has a conventional bullet shape, with pointed ogival nose-cone.

## ENGINES

Polaris A2 has Aerojet-General solid-propellent motors, each with four nozzles. First stage incorporates 'jetevator' controls to steer missile; second stage has gimballed nozzles. Polaris A3 has Aerojet-General first-stage motor with four gimballed nozzles and Hercules second-stage motor with thrust deflection for steering.

## GUIDANCE

Inertial system, produced by General Electric and Hughes.

## WARHEAD

Thermonuclear (H-bomb) type.

## DIMENSIONS

*Length:* 31′.
*Body diameter:* 4′ 6″.

## WEIGHT (approx)

30,000 lb.

## PERFORMANCE

*Range:* A2 1,700 miles, A3 2,875 miles.
*Speed:* 6,600 m.p.h.

**Perfection of this missile represents one of the greatest achievements in missile engineering. The problem presented to Lockheed and their subcontractors in 1956 was to produce an H-bomb missile small enough to be carried in quantity by a submarine and able to be launched underwater. They succeeded so well that eight Polaris submarines, each armed with 16 missiles, were in commission by the spring of 1962. Today there are 41. Polaris is forced out of its vertical storage tube in the submarine by a small solid-propellent rocket. Its first-stage motor fires as soon as it breaks clear of the surface of the sea. Thirteen submarines are armed with UGM–27B Polaris A2, the rest with UGM–27C A3 missiles. The Royal Navy has four A3-equipped submarines.**

# QUAIL (ADM–20) (U.S.A.)

Air-launched decoy missile

*Built by*: McDonnell Aircraft Corporation

## CONFIGURATION

This small and unique missile is made largely of reinforced plastics. It has a rectangular-section body, with side intakes for the turbojet in the rear. There are two pairs of fins above and below the stubby wings, the complete wing-fin assemblies being designed to fold flat against the sides and bottom of the body when the Quail is stowed in the bomb-bay of its launch aircraft.

## ENGINE

One 2,450-lb.s.t. General Electric J85–GE–7 turbojet.

## GUIDANCE

By McDonnell-designed automatic pilot.

## WARHEAD

None.

## DIMENSIONS

*Length*: 12′ 10″. *Wing span*: 5′ 4″.
*Height*: 3′ 4″.

## WEIGHT

1,230 lb.

## PERFORMANCE

*Speed:* over 600 m.p.h.
*Range:* 345 miles.

**Quail is unique in that it does not attack anything, but is designed to protect the B–52 Stratofortress bombers of the U.S.A.F. from enemy fighters and missiles. Its small airframe is packed with electronic and other devices to confuse and jam the enemy defences. Details are secret, but it has been announced that the five-foot span Quail produces the same-size ‘ blip ’ on a radar screen as does the 185-foot span B–52.**

**Quails are stowed in pairs inside the bomb bay, with their wings and fins folded. When released, their wings open out automatically and they fly a carefully planned course of more than three hundred miles. They have been operational with Strategic Air Command since the spring of 1961. The current version is designated ADM–20C.**

GAM-72
U.S. AIR FORCE

## **R.530** (France)

Air-to-air guided missile

*Built by:* S.A. Engins Matra

### CONFIGURATION

Cylindrical body and slightly tapered nose. Four fixed delta wings mid-way-back on body. Control surfaces consist of ailerons on two of the wings and four movable tail-fins. Infra-red version has glass nose window.

### ENGINE

Dual-thrust Hotchkiss-Brandt solid-propellent rocket motor, giving 18,740 lb.s.t.

### GUIDANCE

Interchangeable semi-active radar or infra-red homing systems.

### WARHEAD

High-explosive type, weighing 60 lb., with proximity fuse.

### DIMENSIONS

*Length:* 10′ 9¼″. *Wing span:* 3′ 7¼″.
*Body diameter:* 10¼″.

### WEIGHT

430 lb.

### PERFORMANCE

*Range:* 11 miles.
*Speed:* 1,800 m.p.h.

**The R.530 has replaced earlier Nord and Matra air-to-air missiles as standard armament on French Air Force and Naval fighters. Versions with both semi-active radar guidance and infra-red homing are operational on Vautours, Mirages and F–8E(FN) Crusaders and also equip Mirages of the Royal Australian, South African and Israeli Air Forces.**

**The version of the R.530 illustrated opposite has semi-active radar guidance, which permits attacks to be made from any direction. Most infra-red homing missiles can be fired only from behind the target, where they pick up most easily the heat from its engine exhaust.**

SNECMA
ATAR 9
MATRA R.530

# RAPIER (Great Britain)

Surface-to-air guided missile

*Built by:* British Aircraft Corporation (Guided Weapons) Ltd.

## CONFIGURATION

Slim cylindrical body with pointed nose-cone. Cruciform cropped-delta wings mid-set on body. Cruciform tail-fins indexed in line with wings.

## ENGINE

IMI solid-propellent rocket motor.

## GUIDANCE

In initial version, the operator aligns an optical sight on the target and then tracks it, using a joystick control. The four-missile launcher follows the tracker automatically in bearing and elevation. The missile is launched at optimum range and is automatically commanded to fly down the optical sight-line to hit the target. Later, Rapier will use a radar tracking system.

## WARHEAD

High-explosive type.

## DIMENSIONS

*Length:* 7′ 3″. *Wing span:* 1′ 3″.
*Body diameter:* 5″.

## WEIGHT

Secret.

## PERFORMANCE

*Range:* about 5 miles.

**This very potent lightweight anti-aircraft missile system was about to enter service with the British Army and Royal Air Force as this book closed for press. The initial version utilises two Land-Rovers. The first tows the launcher-trailer and carries the optical tracker, radio equipment, four missiles in sealed containers and three members of the launch crew. The second Land-Rover tows a trailer carrying nine more missiles and carries additional equipment plus the remaining two crew members. The tracker is normally removed from the Land-Rover and ' sits ' on a tripod when deployed for action, but it can remain on the vehicle, which reduces the into-action time of the missiles and provides weather protection for the operator. In early firing trials, Rapiers destroyed small targets travelling at high speed and low altitude nearly two miles from their launchers.**

# REDEYE (MIM–43A) (U.S.A.)

Infantry surface-to-air guided missile

*Built by:* General Dynamics/Pomona

## CONFIGURATION

The Redeye is a slim cylindrical missile consisting of a solid-propellent motor, warhead and infra-red guidance package. It is transported inside its launching tube, which is fitted with a sling like that of a rifle. As it leaves the tube, its small nose-vanes and cruciform tail-fins flip open.

## ENGINE

Dual-thrust solid-propellent rocket motor produced by Atlantic Research Corporation.

## GUIDANCE

Infra-red homing system, housed behind glass nose of missile.

## WARHEAD

High-explosive type.

## DIMENSIONS

*Length:* 4′. *Body diameter:* $2\frac{3}{4}$″.

## WEIGHT

20 lb.

## PERFORMANCE

Secret.

**The Redeye was developed in an effort to provide infantry units of the U.S. Army and Marine Corps with individual protection against low-flying enemy ground attack aircraft. It is a Bazooka-type weapon, fired from the shoulder, and is light enough to be carried in the same way as a rifle. On sighting an approaching enemy aircraft, the operator ‘ warms up ’ the missile's guidance system. A buzzer tells him when it is ready to fire. He tracks the target by use of a monocular sight and when it is within range fires the Redeye, which is propelled out of the launch tube by its booster charge. When it has travelled about 20 ft. (far enough to protect the operator from blast) the main rocket stage ignites and the missile homes on its target. It entered first-line service in 1967 and will also equip the Swedish and Australian armies.**

## RED TOP (Great Britain)

Air-to-air guided missile

*Built by:* Hawker Siddeley Dynamics Ltd.

### CONFIGURATION

Cylindrical body. Hemispherical nose, covering the infra-red guidance unit. Four fixed wings, well back on body. Four tail control surfaces, indexed in line with wings.

### ENGINE

Solid-propellent rocket motor.

### GUIDANCE

Infra-red homing.

### WARHEAD

High-explosive type, weighing 68 lb. Detonated by proximity fuse.

### DIMENSIONS

*Length:* 11′ 5¾″. *Wing span:* 2′ 11¾″.
*Body diameter:* 8¾″.

### WEIGHT

Secret.

### PERFORMANCE

*Range:* 7 miles. *Speed:* 2,000 m.p.h.

**Red Top is a greatly improved development of H.S.D.'s Firestreak air-to-air missile and was, in fact, known originally as Firestreak Mk. 4. The general layout of the missile has been made more logical, with the warhead in the front, near to the fuse; and there is an all-round increase in performance. A larger motor gives higher speed, and the larger wings give greatly improved manoeuvrability, especially at height. Most important of all, the new infra-red guidance system is so sensitive that Red Top can be fired at the target from any direction, instead of only from astern. It equips the later Marks of Lightning interceptor in service with R.A.F. Strike Command, and the Royal Navy's Sea Vixen F.(AW) Mk. 2.**

STBD

# ROBOT RB04 (Sweden)

Air-to-surface guided missile

*Developed by:* Robotavdelningen (Guided Weapons Directorate), Royal Swedish Air Force Board

## CONFIGURATION

Bullet-shape body, with mid-set wings mounted at rear. Fixed fins at wing-tips. Control surfaces comprise four movable fore-planes on nose and ailerons in wing trailing-edges.

## ENGINE

Solid-propellent rocket motor.

## GUIDANCE

High-efficiency homing system.

## WARHEAD

High-explosive type, weighing approx. 660 lb.

## DIMENSIONS

*Length:* 14′ 7″. *Wing span:* 6′ 8½″. *Body diameter:* 1′ 7½″.

## WEIGHT

1,320 lb.

## PERFORMANCE

Secret.

**Intended mainly for attacking targets at sea, in all weathers, this missile has been operational on Saab A32A Lansen two-seat fighters of the Royal Swedish Air Force since early 1959. Each aircraft carries two, on underwing pylons, the latest version being designated RB04D.**

**Development of the Robot RB04 started in 1950, following firing tests of an earlier experimental missile designated Robot 302. The first full-size airframe was flight tested in the spring of 1954, and the first complete Robot RB04 was launched successfully from a Saab J29 single-seat fighter on February 11, 1955. An improved RB04E version is under development by Saab and will equip Sweden's new AJ37 Viggen supersonic attack aircraft.**

L
15

# SAAB RB08A (Sweden)

Ship-to-ship or surface-to-ship guided missile

*Built by:* Saab Aktiebolag

## CONFIGURATION

Aeroplane layout, with circular-section fuselage, mid-set sweptback wings and sweptback 'Y' type tail surfaces. Nose radome above semi-circular air intake. End-plate on each wingtip. Missile is launched on carriage powered by two solid-propellent booster rockets, as shown in illustration opposite. Steered in flight by spoilers on wings and by tail control surfaces.

## ENGINE

Turboméca Marboré IID turbojet sustainer. Two solid-propellent jettisonable boosters.

## GUIDANCE

Stabilised during initial phase of flight. Terminal homing.

## WARHEAD

Highly effective high-explosive type of Swedish design.

## DIMENSIONS

*Length:* 18′ 9″. *Wing span:* 9′ 10½″ *Body diameter:* 2′ 2″.

## WEIGHT

1,985 lb.

## PERFORMANCE

Secret.

**This very effective weapon has been developed by Saab from the French Aérospatiale (Nord) CT.20 target drone, specifically for defence against invasion from the sea. Work on the project began in 1959 and progressed so well that the Royal Swedish Navy placed a large development and production contract for the RB08A in 1965. The weapon is deployed mainly on naval destroyers, but can also be launched from shore bases. Its wings fold for stowage and transport. Performance is secret but the CT.20 drone has a top speed of 560 m.p.h. and endurance of up to one hour**

## ' SANDAL ' (Russia)

Surface-to-surface bombardment missile

**CONFIGURATION**

Cylindrical body, with flared skirt around rocket nozzle and a conical nose-cone. Four small tail-fins, each with a control surface hinged to its trailing-edge and linked with control vanes operating in the rocket exhaust.

**ENGINE**

One liquid-propellent rocket engine, probably developed from the wartime V–2 engine. No booster.

**GUIDANCE**

Unknown, but probably some form of radio-inertial guidance.

**WARHEAD**

Almost certainly alternative nuclear or high-explosive types.

**DIMENSIONS (approx)**

*Length:* 68′. *Body diameter:* 5′ 3″.

**WEIGHT (estimated)**

60,000 lb.

**PERFORMANCE (estimated)**

*Range:* 1,100 miles.
*Speed:* 4,300 m.p.h.

**A regular exhibit in military parades through Moscow since 1957, this was the first large Russian rocket displayed in public and was almost certainly developed from the wartime German V.2, with a similar type of engine. It is always shown on a wheeled transporter, towed by a tracked vehicle containing the launch crew.**

**The original version was about 60 ft. long and had larger tail-fins, but lacked the flared skirt around the jet nozzle. It was known to NATO as ' Shyster '. The current version (' Sandal ') is the missile that caused an international crisis when it was deployed briefly in Cuba in 1962.**

# ' SAVAGE ' (SS–13) (Russia)

Surface-to-surface intercontinental ballistic missile

## CONFIGURATION

Three-stage missile. All stages are cylindrical, of progressively smaller diameter, and are separated by open truss structures. The four nozzles of each stage are covered by a flared skirt. The third stage has a pointed nose-cone.

## ENGINES

All three stages are powered by a solid-propellent rocket motor with four nozzles.

## GUIDANCE

Unknown.

## WARHEAD

Almost certainly nuclear or thermonuclear.

## DIMENSIONS (approx)

*Length:* 66′ *Body diameter:* first stage 5′ 6″, second 4′ 7½″, third 3′ 2½″.

## WEIGHT AND PERFORMANCE

Secret.

**Russia's counterpart to Minuteman, this is the most advanced Soviet strategic bombardment missile yet displayed publicly. The inter-stage truss structure, inherited from ' Scrag ', may appear strange to Western eyes, but it is entirely practical and simple. The trolley on which the weapon is displayed is only a transporter, and ' Savage ' is almost certainly stored in, and fired from an underground ' silo ' to reduce its vulnerability to an enemy first strike. Depending on the efficiency of its solid propellents, its range might be anything from 2,000 to 5,000 miles. It was first seen in May 1965.**

## ' SCALEBOARD ' (Russia)

Surface-to-surface tactical missile

### CONFIGURATION

The precise configuration of this weapon is not known, as it has never been displayed or photographed without the ribbed container in which it is stowed on its wheeled transporter-launch vehicle. From the shape of the container it would appear that the missile is very similar in layout to the smaller ' Scud–B ', with a cylindrical body, pointed nose-cone and cruciform tail-fins. However, the shape of the fairings over the base of the missile could suggest the presence of vernier engines rather than fins.

### ENGINE

Probably storable liquid-propellent rocket motor.

### GUIDANCE

Unknown, but set up on console mounted between inner wheels in port side of transporter.

### WARHEAD

Almost certainly nuclear.

### DIMENSION (estimated)

*Length:* 37′.

### WEIGHT

Unknown.

### PERFORMANCE (estimated)

*Range:* 450 miles.

**The original ' Scud–A ' tactical bombardment missile, carried on a tracked launcher, has been in standard service with the armies of Russia and its Allies for many years. The larger ' Scud–B ', carried on a new wheeled erector-launcher, was first displayed publicly in November 1965. Two years later ' Scaleboard ' put in an appearance on the same wheeled transporter-launcher. Larger than the ' Scuds ' it is, like them, a guided bombardment missile and can be expected to become a standard weapon of the Soviet Army.**

# ‘SCAMP/SCAPEGOAT’ (Russia)

Mobile surface-to-surface bombardment missile

## CONFIGURATION

Two-stage missile, consisting of the top two stages of the SS–13 ‘Savage’ ICBM, with open truss structure between stages. Always transported inside ‘Scamp’ container.

## ENGINE

Two-stage solid-propellent rocket motors, with four nozzles on each stage.

## GUIDANCE

Unknown.

## WARHEAD

Almost certainly nuclear or thermonuclear.

## DIMENSIONS (estimated)

*Length:* 35′. *Body diameter:* first stage 4′ 7½″, second 3′ 2½″.

## WEIGHT

Unknown.

## PERFORMANCE (estimated)

*Range:* 2,500 miles.

**When Western observers first saw this mobile strategic missile in a Moscow parade, on May 9, 1965, they immediately nicknamed it ‘the Iron Maiden’ because of the way the missile is enclosed in a container made in two halves and hinged horizontally. The NATO code-name ‘Scamp’ applies to the entire weapon system, including the tracked transporter-erector-launch vehicle. Photographs have shown that, in action, the missile (‘Scapegoat’), still in its container, is raised to a vertical position above the firing platform at the rear of the vehicle. The container is then opened up and moved away before the missile is launched. ‘Scamp’ is best regarded as a kind of land-based Polaris. It has a big brother, known to NATO as ‘Scrooge’, which is transported in, and fired from, a 62 ft.-long cylindrical container on a similar tracked transporter-erector-launch vehicle.**

# ‘SCARP’ (Russia)

Intercontinental ballistic missile and FOBS launch vehicle

## CONFIGURATION

Long cylindrical body, joined to slim cylindrical re-entry vehicle by tapered fairing. Four wedge-shape fairings over vernier engines at tail.

## ENGINES

First-stage liquid-propellent propulsion system has six nozzles, with four vernier nozzles faired into the periphery of the surrounding skirt.

## GUIDANCE

Unknown.

## WARHEAD

Standard SS–9 ICBM has either a 20/25-megaton thermonuclear warhead or multiple re-entry vehicles (MRV). Alternative version carries FOBS ‘space bomb’ warhead, as described below.

## DIMENSIONS

*Length:* 113′ 6″. *Body diameter:* 10′.

## WEIGHT AND PERFORMANCE

Unknown.

**First shown in a Moscow parade on November 7, 1967, marking the 50th anniversary of the Communist Revolution, ‘Scarp’ carries a heavier warhead than any known ICBM. More than 275 of the standard ICBMs, designated SS–9, were in service at the beginning of 1970, some with three-warhead MRVs. These are expected to be evolved into multiple independently-targeted re-entry vehicles (MIRVs) which will be able to explode in a ‘footprint’ matching precisely the distances between a cluster of three U.S. Minuteman ICBM silo launchers. One MRV was photographed from a U.S. reconnaissance aircraft over the Pacific as the three warheads re-entered the atmosphere 5,500 miles from the missile launch site. In addition to the SS–9, a version of ‘Scarp’ is used to launch Russia's Fractional Orbital Bombardment System (FOBS) ‘space bomb’. This version puts an H-bomb warhead into low orbit, about 100 miles above the Earth. Then, at a predetermined point, during the first orbit, a retro-rocket slows the warhead and causes it to drop on its target.**

## **SEACAT** (Great Britain)

Surface-to-air ship-launched guided missile

*Built by*: Short Brothers & Harland, Ltd.

### CONFIGURATION

Basically cylindrical body, enlarged to an almost square section where the four pivoted sweptback wings are attached. Four fixed tail-fins, indexed at 45° to wings. Two fins carry tracking flares at their tips.

### ENGINE

Dual-thrust solid-propellent rocket motor.

### GUIDANCE

Radio command type. With the Mk. 20 director unit, one man rotates the director so that the second man (the aimer) can pick up the target visually and follow it through binoculars. The quadruple missile launcher is linked to turn with the director, so the missile soon enters the aimer's field of view after it is fired. The aimer then guides it into the target by movements of a miniature joystick. Alternatively the ship can be fitted with a Mk. 21 or 22 close-range blind-firing radar director or the Dutch M4-3 one-man radar-controlled director. Other systems include one that replaces optical aiming with a closed-circuit TV system.

### WARHEAD

Large high-explosive type, with both proximity and impact fuses.

### DIMENSIONS

*Length:* 4′ 10″. *Wing span:* 2′ 1½″. *Body diameter:* 7.5″.

### WEIGHT AND PERFORMANCE

Secret.

**This highly efficient close-range anti-aircraft missile entered service with the Royal Navy in the summer of 1962 and now equips many ships, including the ' County ' class of fleet escort super-destroyers and destroyers of the ' Battle ' and ' Leander ' classes. It has been ordered also for ships of the Argentinian, Australian, Iranian, New Zealand, Netherlands, Malaysian, Swedish, Chilean, Brazilian, Indian, Libyan, Venezuelan and West German Navies. Seacat's main job is to provide a last-ditch defence against aircraft that have broken through the Fleet's shield of fighter aircraft and long-range missiles, but it can also be used in a surface-to-surface role. A lightweight three-round launcher is available for small ships, and a land-based version, known as Tigercat, is in production for the Royal Air Force Regiment, Iran, Jordan and Qatar.**

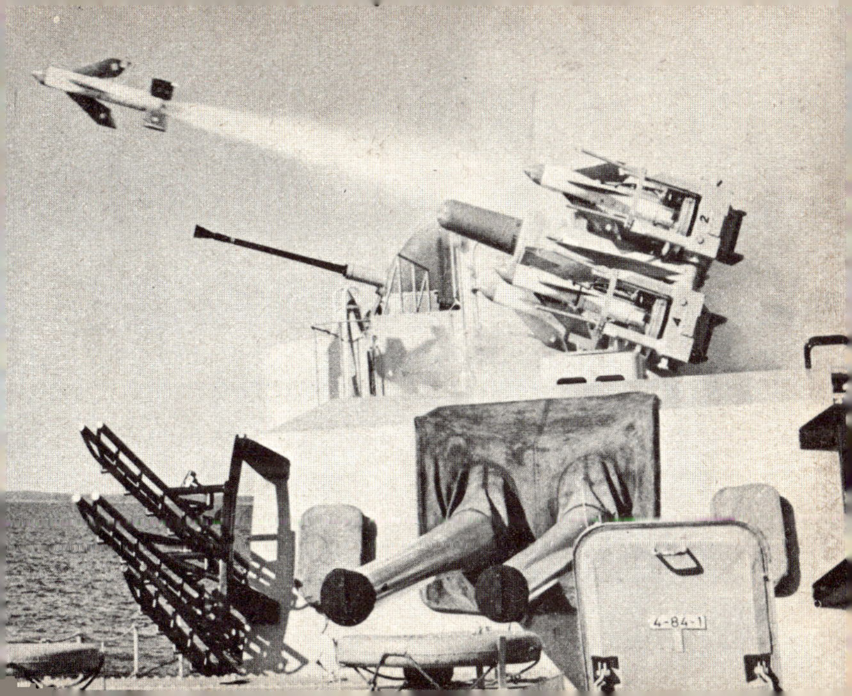
4-84-1

# SEASLUG (Great Britain)

Surface-to-air ship-launched guided missile

*Built by:* Hawker Siddeley Dynamics Ltd.

## CONFIGURATION

Basic missile has slim cylindrical body, with pointed nose-cone. Four fixed wings are mounted more than half-way back on the body. Four pivoted tail control surfaces are indexed in line with the wings. To keep the length and diameter of the missile as small as possible, for shipboard stowage, the four boosters are ' wrapped ' round the front of the body, where they need no stabilising fins.

## ENGINES

One I.C.I. solid-propellent rocket motor in body. Four solid-propellent boosters which jettison after burn-out.

## GUIDANCE

Beam-riding guidance, by General Electric Co. and Sperry.

## WARHEAD

High-explosive type, with proximity fuse.

## DIMENSIONS

*Length:* 20′. *Wing span:* 4′ 8½″.
*Body diameter:* 1′ 4″.

## WEIGHT AND PERFORMANCE

Secret.

**Tests of this long-range anti-aircraft missile from H.M.S. ' Girdle Ness ' proved so successful that there was a shortage of target aircraft and the later rounds had to be set to miss by a predetermined distance. Canberra pilotless target aircraft have been destroyed at well over 50,000 ft. Other fast-flying targets have been brought down at very low levels, and Seaslug has been called the best shipborne missile in the world. Seaslug Mk. 2 is primary armament on the eight ' County ' class fleet escort super-destroyers of the Royal Navy. Compared with the original Seaslug Mk. 1, which it replaced, it offers longer range, even better performance against low-flying aircraft and suitability for use in a surface-to-surface role.**

# SERGEANT (MGM-29A) (U.S.A.)

Surface-to-surface field artillery guided missile

*Built by:* Sperry/Univac Salt Lake City

## CONFIGURATION

Cylindrical body, with fairly long pointed nose-cone. Four fixed tail-fins with small control surfaces hinged to their trailing-edges and linked to jet-deflection vanes operating in the rocket exhaust.

## ENGINE

One 55,000-lb.s.t. Thiokol M100 solid-propellent rocket motor. No booster.

## GUIDANCE

Inertial system produced by Univac SLC.

## WARHEAD

Alternative nuclear or high-explosive types.

## DIMENSIONS

*Length:* 34′ 6″. *Fin span:* 5′ 10¼″. *Body diameter:* 2′ 7″.

## WEIGHT

10,100 lb.

## PERFORMANCE

*Range:* 29–86 miles. *Speed:* 2,300 m.p.h.

**Sergeant was developed for the U.S. Army as a replacement for the liquid-propellent Corporal. Its design was started in 1956 and it became operational in 1962. Sergeant itself, and all items of support equipment, can be transported in U.S.A.F. aircraft and on standard Army vehicles. In the combat area, it can be emplaced and fired in under thirty minutes by a six-man crew, an unusual feature being that it is launched at an angle of 75° as shown in the illustration opposite. Sergeant is also in service with the West German armed forces. A complete battery is transported on three semi-trailers and one standard 2½-ton truck.**

US ARMY

# SHILLELAGH (MGM–51A) (U.S.A.)

Lightweight close-support army missile

*Built by:* Philco-Ford Corporation

## CONFIGURATION

Torpedo-shape body, with four tail fins which fold around the body in the launch-tube and flip open in flight.

## ENGINE

Amoco Chemicals solid-propellent rocket motor.

## GUIDANCE

Philco-Ford command guidance system. Missile follows a line-of-sight from the gunner to the target. Gunner has only to keep the cross-hairs of his optical sight aligned on target and Shillelagh follows automatically.

## WARHEAD

Octol shaped charge.

## DIMENSIONS

*Length:* 3′ 9″. *Body diameter:* 6″.

## WEIGHT

60 lb.

## PERFORMANCE

*Range:* about 10 miles.

**Shillelagh was developed to provide greatly increased fire-power against enemy armour, troops and fortifications in battle. It is launched from a dual-purpose gun-launcher, which can also fire conventional ammunition of the same (152-mm.) diameter. Initially, the gun-launcher was mounted on the U.S. Army's new General Sheridan armoured reconnaissance and airborne assault vehicle, and Shillelagh entered service in this form in 1967. It will also be carried by the Army's M60 A1E2 battle tank and by the U.S.-West German 'Main Battle Tank' when this becomes operational in the early 1970's.**

# SIDEWINDER (AIM–9) (U.S.A.)

Air-to-air guided missile

*Built by*: Philco-Ford Corporation and General Electric Co. in the U.S.A., Bodenseewerk Perkin-Elmer in Germany

## CONFIGURATION

Slim cylindrical body, with spherical glass nose over infra-red guidance unit. Four small pivoted control surfaces on nose. Four fixed tail-fins indexed in line with control surfaces.

## ENGINE

Naval Propellant Plant solid-propellent rocket motor.

## GUIDANCE

Infra-red homing system by Philco.

## WARHEAD

High-explosive type, weighing about 25 lb.

## DIMENSIONS (AIM–9B)

*Length:* 9′ 3½″. *Fin span:* 1′ 10″.
*Body diameter:* 5″.

## WEIGHT (AIM–9B)

159 lb.

## PERFORMANCE

*Range:* 2 miles. *Speed:* 1,600 m.p.h

**Altogether, well over 50,000 AIM–9B Sidewinder 1A's were produced in America for the U.S. Air Force, Navy and Marine Corps, the Royal Navy, Royal Canadian Navy and the Air Forces of about 15 other countries. Many more have been built in Europe. They are extremely simple, containing fewer than two dozen moving parts and no more electronic components than a home radio set. An improved version known as Sidewinder 1C, with higher speed, longer range and interchangeable infra-red (AIM–9D) and semi-active radar (AIM–9C) homing heads, is in production to arm the F–8 Crusader fighter and other types. It is also used in surface-to-air form in the U.S. Army's Chaparral battlefield defence system. Two standard Sidewinder 1A's are shown opposite on the wing-tips of a Lockheed F–104 Starfighter.**

6748
FG-748
U.S. AIR FORCE

## ‘ SNAPPER ’ (Russia)

Light anti-tank guided missile

**CONFIGURATION**

Cylindrical body, with warhead in pointed nose-cone. Four fixed wings, each with a vibrating spoiler in the trailing-edge for control purposes.

**ENGINE**

Solid-propellent rocket motor.

**GUIDANCE**

Conventional wire guidance.

**WARHEAD**

Hollow-charge high-explosive type, weighing 11.5 lb.

**DIMENSIONS**

*Length:* 3′ 8½″. *Wing span:* 2′ 6″.
*Body diameter:* 5½″.

**WEIGHT**

49 lb.

**PERFORMANCE**

*Range:* 550–2,550 yards.
*Speed:* 201 m.p.h.

**First of a series of small solid-propellen anti-tank missiles to become standard equip ment with the Soviet armed forces, ‘ Snapper is similar in configuration to Western missile such as the Bölkow Cobra and earlier Nor SS.10. It is normally deployed, as illustrate opposite, on a triple mounting carried by BRDM armoured amphibious vehicle. Thi mounting is retractable, so that the missile are protected by cover plates when not re quired for action.**

**As examples of ‘ Snapper ’ were capture by the Israeli forces in Sinai in 1967, th missile has clearly been exported to Russia’ friends and allies. In the Red Army, it i supplemented by a larger missile (NATC code-name ‘ Swatter ’), in the class of th French SS.11, and by a much more compac missile (‘ Sagger ’) first seen in 1965 an carried in clutches of six by the BRDN vehicle.**

# SPARROW IIIB (AIM–7E) (U.S.A.)

Air-to-air guided missile

*Built by:* Raytheon Co.

## CONFIGURATION

Slim cylindrical body with curved nose-cone. Four pivoted wings, mid-way back on body, are used for controlling the missile's flight path. Four fixed tail-fins indexed in line with wings.

## ENGINE

Rocketdyne Mk. 38 Mod. 2 solid-propellent rocket motor.

## GUIDANCE

Raytheon continuous-wave semi-active radar homing system.

## WARHEAD

High-explosive type, reported to weigh 60 lb.

## DIMENSIONS

*Length:* 12′. *Wing span:* 3′ 4″. *Body diameter:* 8″.

## WEIGHT

450 lb.

## PERFORMANCE

*Range:* over 8 miles. *Speed:* over 2,300 m.p.h.

**Sparrow IIIB is one of the largest air-to-air missiles in service outside Russia, with a very heavy warhead. It can be used in all weathers and at all altitudes, even against targets that are seen by the pilot only as a ' blip ' on a radar screen.**

**Two factories, at South Lowell, Massachusetts, and Bristol, Tennessee, are engaged on production of Sparrow IIIB, which became operational on fighters of the U.S. Navy in August 1958. Sparrow IIIB's form the main armament of the McDonnell Douglas Phantom II fighters of the U.S. Navy, U.S.A.F., Royal Air Force, Royal Navy and other air forces and the Italian Air Force's Lockheed F–104S Starfighters.**

**A ship-launched surface-to-air version, known as Sea Sparrow, is operational on vessels of the U.S., Canadian and NATO navies, for close-range defence against aircraft and missiles.**

R-1060

# SRAM (AGM–69A) (U.S.A.)

Air-to-surface guided missile

*Built by:* The Boeing Company

## CONFIGURATION

Basically cylindrical body, with long ogival nose-cone and three tail control surfaces equi-spaced around rocket nozzle. Nozzle covered by jettisonable tapered tail fairing in flight to streamline missile.

## ENGINE

Lockheed Propulsion Company restartable solid-propellent pulse rocket motor.

## GUIDANCE

General Precision inertial system.

## WARHEAD

Nuclear or high-explosive, as required.

## DIMENSIONS

*Length:* 14′. *Body diameter:* 1′ 5½″.

## WEIGHT

Approx. 2,240 lb.

## PERFORMANCE (estimated)

*Range:* 140 miles.

**SRAM, America's new air-launched short-range attack missile is designed to travel at supersonic speed and to penetrate the most advanced enemy defensive systems. It is said to appear no larger than a much slower machine-gun bullet on a radar screen. Up to 20 SRAMs will be carried by Strategic Air Command's big B–52G and H Stratofortress bombers; each of its smaller swing-wing FB–111s will carry up to six of the missiles. After launch, each missile will follow a pre-set unjammable course to its target, travelling just above the ground, in a high ballistic trajectory or an intermediate 'dog leg' course, as considered most effective by the attackers. Development of the SRAM was started in 1966. First flight trials from a B–52 in 1969 were successful and the missile was planned to become operational in 1972.**

## SS.11 and AS.11 (Nord 5210) (France)

Anti-tank guided missile

*Built by:* Société Nationale Industrielle Aérospatiale

### CONFIGURATION

Cylindrical body, with warhead in rounded nose-section. Four fixed sweptback wings.

### ENGINE

Dual-thrust solid-propellent rocket motor.

### GUIDANCE

Conventional wire guidance. Missile is spin-stabilised and is steered in flight by varying the thrust of the rocket exhaust through the two side nozzles.

### WARHEAD

Variety of high-explosive, armour-piercing and high-fragmentation anti-personnel types.

### DIMENSIONS

*Length:* 3′ 11″. *Wing span:* 1′ 7½″. *Body diameter:* 6½″.

### WEIGHT

66 lb.

### PERFORMANCE

*Range:* 550–3,280 yards.
*Speed:* 360 m.p.h.

**The SS.11 is considerably larger and more powerful than the original Nord SS.10, which pioneered the modern concept of wire-guided anti-tank missiles, and has one warhead capable of penetrating 24 in. of steel plate. It is too heavy for easy man-handling by infantry, but is widely used as a vehicle-mounted weapon by all three French services and the armies of many other countries. The AS.11 air-to-surface version has been fitted to several types of French aircraft and is standard armament on the Westland Wessex assault helicopters of the Royal Navy.**

**More than 140,000 SS.11's and AS.11's have been built for delivery to 21 countries. A new version, named the Harpon, was introduced in 1967, for carriage by the French AMX tank and other vehicles. With this, the operator keeps an optical sight aimed on the target and the missile is then held on course automatically by infra-red guidance.**

823361

# **SS.12** (France)

Wire-guided surface-to-surface tactical missile

*Built by:* Société Nationale Industrielle Aérospatiale

## CONFIGURATION

Basically cylindrical body, with warhead in bulged nose section. Four fixed wings.

## ENGINE

Dual-thrust solid-propellent rocket motor.

## GUIDANCE

Conventional wire guidance. Missile is spin-stabilised and is steered in flight by varying the thrust of the rocket exhaust through the two side nozzles. It can utilise the optical aiming/infra-red guidance system used with the Harpon and described under the SS.11 entry on page 102.

## WARHEAD

High-explosive, armour-piercing or anti-personnel type, weighing up to 66 lb.

## DIMENSIONS

*Length:* 6′ 2″. *Wing span:* 2′ 1½″.
*Body diameter:* 7″.

## WEIGHT

167 lb.

## PERFORMANCE

*Range:* 3¾ miles. *Speed:* 450 m.p.h.

**Taking advantage of the success of the SS.11, Nord produced this larger weapon on the same lines, but with a warhead about four times as heavy as that of the SS.11. It is suitable for battle area use from vehicles against tanks and static targets. A slightly modified version, designated AS.12, is being produced for air-to-surface use and is carried by Breguet Alizé carrier-based anti-submarine aircraft and land-based Breguet Atlantics of the French Navy, and by Neptunes of the Royal Netherlands Navy. A marine version, the SS.12M, is available to arm fast naval patrol boats.**

# STANDARD MISSILE (RIM-66A/67A) (U.S.A.)

Surface-to-air guided missile

*Built by:* General Dynamics Corporation

## CONFIGURATION

Cylindrical body, with pointed nose-cone. Four short-span wings of very long chord, with halved span on leading sections. Cruciform tail control surfaces indexed in line with wings. Extended-range RIM-67A version has added first-stage booster, with cylindrical body and four tail-fins indexed in line with fins of second stage.

## ENGINES

RIM-66A has Aerojet dual-thrust solid-propellent rocket motor. RIM-67A has two solid-propellent stages supplied by Atlantic Research and the Naval Propellent Plant.

## GUIDANCE

Semi-active radar homing system by General Dynamics Pomona.

## WARHEAD

High-explosive type.

## DIMENSIONS

*Length:* RIM-66A over 14′, RIM-67A over 26′.

## WEIGHT

RIM-66A 1,300 lb., RIM-67A 3,000 lb.

## PERFORMANCE

*Range:* RIM-66A over 15 miles, RIM-67A over 35 miles.

**Standard Missile was conceived as a replacement for the earlier Tartar and Terrier which arm a very large number of ships of the U.S. Navy and others of the French, Italian, Japanese, Royal Netherlands and Royal Australian Navies. The two versions are similar in external appearance to the missiles they supersede, but offer improved performance and reliability. Development began in 1964 and production has been under way for several years, with the aim of equipping a total of more than 50 American destroyers, frigates and escort vessels. Only minor changes are needed to launch and control systems already installed for earlier weapons. The RIM-66A medium-range version of Standard Missile forms the basis of the air-to-surface Standard ARM, which is superseding Shrike as a homing weapon to knock out enemy radars, and Aegis, the U.S. Navy's new advanced surface-to-air missile system. Standard Missiles can also be used in a surface-to-surface role.**

## 'STYX' (Russia)

Ship-launched surface-to-surface 'flying bomb' missile

### CONFIGURATION

Aeroplane layout, with a cylindrical body, mid-set cropped-delta wings and three identical tail surfaces, each consisting of a fixed fin and trailing-edge control surface. Almost full-span ailerons on wings. Jettisonable booster rocket is carried under rear fuselage.

### ENGINES

Sustainer rocket engine nozzle in tail of missile. Solid-propellent booster rocket falls away after burn-out.

### GUIDANCE

Unknown, but believed to be of radar homing type.

### WARHEAD

High-explosive type.

### DIMENSIONS (approx.)

*Length:* 20′. *Body diameter:* 2′ 3″. *Wing span:* 8′ 10″.

### WEIGHT

Secret.

### PERFORMANCE

*Range:* at least 15 miles.

**This is one of several 'flying bomb' cruise missiles currently in service with the Soviet armed forces. It is standard armament on Soviet fast patrol boats, two being carried by ships of the 'Komar' class and four by 'Osa' class ships. 'Styx' is housed inside a small hangar and fired from a twin-rail launcher built into the hangar. It is in service also with the navies of Cuba, Egypt and many other countries, and the Egyptians used 'Styx' missiles from an 'Osa' class ship to sink the Israeli destroyer 'Eilat' on October 21, 1967. Larger and more advanced missiles of this type are carried by Russia's 'Krupnyi', 'Kanin' and 'Kotlin' class destroyers.**

# SUBROC (UUM-44A) (U.S.A.)

Underwater-to-underwater guided missile

*Built by*: Goodyear Aerospace Corporation

## CONFIGURATION

Subroc consists of a torpedo-shape depth bomb warhead, mounted on the nose of a first-stage solid-propellent booster rocket of larger diameter. The warhead is fitted with a short ogival nose-cone and four tail control surfaces.

## ENGINE

Thiokol solid-propellent rocket motor of booster has four nozzles with jet-deflection system for steering the missile both underwater and in the air.

## GUIDANCE

General Precision inertial type.

## WARHEAD

Nuclear depth bomb.

## DIMENSIONS (approx)

*Length:* 21′. *Maximum body diameter:* 1′ 9″.

## WEIGHT (approx)

4,000 lb.

## PERFORMANCE (estimated)

*Range:* 25–30 miles.

**Subroc (submarine rocket) is unique, in that it is designed to be launched underwater, from the normal torpedo tubes of a submarine, and then to travel through the air at supersonic speed before re-entering the water to attack an enemy submarine. The booster motor ignites when the missile is well clear of the launch-submarine, which can be moving and need not be pointing towards the target. Subroc's course can be changed underwater, as it is propelled upward and into the air. At a predetermined distance, the rocket motor is separated from the nuclear depth bomb by thrust-reversal. The inertial guidance system continues to direct the missile to the target area, steering it by means of the tail fins. This determines the position and angle of the missile as it re-enters the water at supersonic speed, to sink and explode. Subroc has been operational in U.S. Navy submarines since late 1965.**

# TALOS (RIM–8) (U.S.A.)

Surface-to-air, ship-launched guided weapon

*Built by:* The Bendix Corporation

## CONFIGURATION

Two-stage missile. The missile itself has a cylindrical body, tapering slightly towards the air intake at the front. Air intake has central shock-cone. The four wings are pivoted for control purposes. Four fixed tail-fins are indexed in line with wings. The cylindrical booster is the same diameter as the missile and is attached in tandem. It too has four tail-fins indexed in line with the wings.

## ENGINES

One 40,000-h.p. Bendix 28-in. ramjet sustainer in missile, running on JP–5 fuel. The jettisonable solid-propellent booster is manufactured by Allegany Ballistics Laboratory.

## GUIDANCE

Beam-riding guidance, with final semi-active homing.

## WARHEAD

There are two versions of Talos, with nuclear and high-explosive warheads respectively. Both are detonated by a proximity fuse.

## DIMENSIONS

*Length:* with booster 38′, withou booster 21′.

*Wing span:* 9′ 6″. *Body diameter:* 2′ 4″

## WEIGHT

With booster 7,800 lb.

## PERFORMANCE

*Range:* over 65 miles.

*Speed:* 1,600 m.p.h.

**Like the British Bloodhound, Talos i ramjet-powered and has a very high perform ance. It is mounted on twin launchers o seven U.S. light and heavy cruisers, includin the nuclear cruiser ‘ Long Beach ’. On thi ship, the fire controller is able to choose th type of warhead he wants, and have th appropriate missile extracted from below-deck stores, raised to its launcher and fired auto matically.**

**Talos missiles fired from the ‘ Long Beach destroyed two MiG fighters over North Vietnam in 1968, about 70 miles from wher they were launched. Latest versions are th RIM–8–G–AAW and RIM–8–H–ARM, th latter for surface-to-surface use against rada sites.**

# THUNDERBIRD (Great Britain)

Mobile surface-to-air guided missile

*Built by:* British Aircraft Corporation (Guided Weapons) Ltd.

## CONFIGURATION

Basic missile is cylindrical, with a pointed nose-cone, four fixed wings mounted well back on the body and four tail control surfaces indexed in line with the wings. Four solid-propellent boosters are ' wrapped ' around the rear of the body, each with a large stabilising fin.

## ENGINES

One solid-propellent rocket sustainer in body. Four jettisonable solid-propellent boosters.

## GUIDANCE

Semi-active homing type, produced by Marconi.

## WARHEAD

High-explosive type, detonated by a proximity fuse.

## DIMENSIONS

*Length:* 20′ 10″. *Wing span:* 5′ 4″. *Body diameter:* 1′ 8¾″.

## WEIGHT AND PERFORMANCE

Secret.

**Thunderbird has been fully operational with anti-aircraft regiments of the Royal Artillery since 1959 and the first overseas unit was sent to form part of the Army of the Rhine in October 1961. It is a mobile weapon, which can be air transported in R.A.F. aircraft, and can be prepared for firing very quickly. The two original regiments have been amalgamated to form one large regiment, No. 36, based in the U.K. but exercising regularly in Germany.**

**The original Thunderbird Mk. 1 has been followed into production and service by the much improved Mk. 2 version with continuous-wave radar guidance, giving greater immunity to jamming and greater effectiveness against low-flying targets. The Mk. 2 began replacing the Mk. 1 at the end of 1965, and some of the earlier missiles have been acquired by the Saudi Arabian government.**

# TITAN 2 (LGM–25C) (U.S.A.)

Intercontinental ballistic missile

*Built by:* Martin Marietta Corporation

## CONFIGURATION

Two-stage missile. Each stage is an aluminium alloy cylinder forming tankage for the rocket propellents and housing the rocket engines. The second stage of Titan 2 has the same diameter as the first and carries at the top the blunt-nosed conical warhead.

## ENGINES

Both stages are powered by an Aerojet-General pre-packaged (storable) liquid-propellent rocket engine. The LR87 first-stage engine gives 430,000 lb.s.t. and has two swivelling nozzles to control the missile's flight path. The LR91 second-stage engine gives 100,000 lb.s.t. and has a single swivelling nozzle. After both engines have stopped, the missile's speed and trajectory are adjusted by four small vernier rockets. The warhead then separates and follows a ballistic trajectory to the target.

## GUIDANCE

Inertial type, produced by AC Electronics.

## WARHEAD

Thermonuclear (H-bomb) type.

## DIMENSIONS

*Length:* 103′.
*Body diameter:* 10′.

## WEIGHT

330,000 lb.

## PERFORMANCE

*Range:* 6,300 miles. *Speed:* 17,000 m.p.h.

**The original Titan 1 was the second of America's big liquid-propellent ICBM's, and began to supplement Atlas squadrons of Strategic Air Command in April 1962. It was followed in 1963 by Titan 2, as described above and illustrated opposite. This is such a formidable weapon that six squadrons, with a total of 54 missiles, have been retained as part of America's nuclear deterrent force even though S.A.C. now has its full quota of 1,000 solid-propellent Minuteman missiles in service. Titan 2's storable liquid-propellent engines permit it to be stored in, and fired from underground 'silo' launchers, like Minuteman. It carries the largest thermonuclear warhead of any U.S. missile.**

AIR
FORCE

## TOW (MGM–71A) (U.S.A.)

Heavy surface-to-surface and air-to-surface anti-tank missile.

*Built by:* Hughes Aircraft Co.

### CONFIGURATION

Cylindrical body with smaller-diameter torpedo-shape nose-cone. Cruciform low aspect-ratio wings, indexed at 45° to cruciform tail control surfaces, all of which remain folded while missile is in launch container and flip out as it leaves.

### ENGINE

Solid-propellent motor, by Hercules Inc., with two separate boost phases so that there is no blast to hurt operator as missile leaves container.

### GUIDANCE

Wire-guided by operator, who simply keeps target centred in telescopic sight.

### WARHEAD

High-explosive shaped charge.

### DIMENSIONS AND PERFORMANCE

Secret, except the range is over one mile.

### WEIGHTS

Missile 48 lb., entire system 200 lb.

**TOW (Tube-launched, Optically-tracked, Wire-guided) is in production to replace the 106 mm recoilless rifle and Entac and SS.11 missiles in U.S. Army service. It will also be fired from two three-missile packs, carried with a stabilised sight, by Army helicopters. TOW is fired on the ground from a tripod-mounted launch tube. It is not handled directly by the firing crew, being inserted into the rear end of the launch-tube inside its transport container, which forms an extension of the tube. Firing trials against moving targets, from both ground launchers and helicopters, have been under way successfully since 1965.**

## VIGILANT (Great Britain)

Infantry anti-tank guided missile

*Built by:* British Aircraft Corporation (Guided Weapons) Ltd.

### CONFIGURATION

Basically cylindrical light alloy body. Four wings of resin-impregnated glass-fibre, with a hinged control surface on the trailing-edge of each.

### ENGINE

Dual-thrust solid-propellent motor manufactured by I.C.I.

### GUIDANCE

Conventional wire guidance. Operator steers the missile by means of a simple thumbstick control unit.

### WARHEAD

High-explosive type, weighing 13.2 lb. and able to penetrate 22 in. of armour plate.

### DIMENSIONS

*Length:* 3′ 6″. *Wing span:* 11″.
*Body diameter:* 4.5″.

### WEIGHT

31 lb.

### PERFORMANCE

*Range:* 250–1,760 yards.
*Speed:* 348 m.p.h.

**Chosen as standard equipment for the British Army, this small anti-tank missile has demonstrated an incredibly high standard of accuracy against moving targets over a wide variety of ranges during firing trials. There is no smoke or flash when it is launched and the small wings enable the missile to be guided past trees and other obstacles with little danger of collision. Operation and steering are so easy that it is not unusual for soldiers to score a direct hit with their first launch. The complete weapon system comprises the missile in its container-launcher, a hand-held sight-controller and connecting cable. It takes less than 30 seconds to get the missile into action and up to six can be operated by one man. Vigilant is also mounted on vehicles such as the Ferret armoured cars of the Royal Armoured Corps. The warhead will penetrate the armour of every known tank. Vigilants have been exported to Finland, Kuwait and Saudi Arabia.**

A TK GM

## OTHER MISSILES, UNDER DEVELOPMENT OR IN SERVICE

**ACRA** (France). Semi-automatic heavy anti-tank missile, fired from gun on armoured vehicle, like American Shillelagh. With a cruising speed two or three times higher than earlier anti-tank rockets, it will penetrate the armour of any known tank over a range of nearly two miles. Cylindrical body, conical nose-cone and four flip-out tail control surfaces.

**'Alkali'** (Russia). Air-to-air missile in standard service. Possibly radar homing.

**'Anab'** (Russia). Standard air-to-air missile. Infra-red and radar homing versions, carried by Su–9 and Yak–28P fighters and the new Su–11.

**AS.20** (France). Small brother of AS.30. See page 4.

**'Ash'** (Russia). Air-to-air. As large as Sparrow, with four big delta wings and four tail surfaces. Radar homing or beam-riding. Probably not in service.

**'Atoll'** (Russia). Almost identical with Sidewinder. Arms MiG–21.

**Bantam** (Sweden). Wire-guided anti-tank missile used by Swiss and Swedish armies. Operated by one man. Glassfibre structure.

**Blowpipe** (G.B.). Bazooka-type surface-to-air, fired by one man. Slim pointed body. Four small foreplanes and rear-mounted fins. Length 53 in. Scheduled to enter production in 1971, including a multiple-launcher version for ships and submarines.

**Chaparral** (U.S.A.). Vehicle-mounted launcher for four Sidewinder ICs in surface-to-air role. In service with U.S. Army.

**Cobra** (Germany). Infantry anti-tank guided missile. Resembles 'Snapper'. More than 100,000 of these lightweight missiles have been built.

**Condor (AGM–53A)** (U.S.A.). Air-to-surface weapon to arm A–6 Intruder and A–7 Corsair II aircraft of U.S. Navy. Resembles enlarged R.530. TV guidance. Range 40 miles.

**Crotale** (France). Under development to intercept supersonic low-flying aircraft. All-weather, radar-directed weapon, with slim pointed body, four foreplanes, four tail-fins. Range 5 miles. Known as Cactus in version for South Africa.

**Dragon (XM47)** (U.S.A.). One-man tube-launched anti-tank missile, resembling Shillelagh. Unique propulsion and steering system uses several pairs of side-thrust rocket motors mounted around body of missile. In early production stage.

**Entac** (France). Typical small wire-guided anti-tank missile. More than 125,000 built for many countries.

**Exocet** (France). Ship-launched surface-to-surface missile designed to knock out enemy vessels before they can launch missiles like ' Styx '. Slim cylindrical body with cruciform delta wings and tail control surfaces. Two-stage solid-propellent motor. Cruises less than 10 ft. above sea at high subsonic speed. Length 16 ft. 9½ in. Range 23 miles. For service from 1971.

**Gabriel** (Israel). Ship-launched surface-to-surface, carried in multiple launchers by Israeli gunboats. Cylindrical body with ogival warhead and large-span unswept cruciform wings. Radar guided. In service.

**' Gainful '** (Russia). Low-altitude solid-propellent surface-to-air rocket missile first displayed in 1967. Three carried atop tracked transporter-launcher. Cylindrical with ogival nose-cone, cruciform wings and tail surfaces. Length about 19 ft. 6 in.

**' Galosh '** (Russia). Anti-missile missile, 65 ft. long. Only seen inside long cylindrical container towed by wheeled tractor. Four first-stage nozzles. In service.

**' Goa ' (SAM–3)** (Russia). Two-stage surface-to-air. Foreplane controls, four rear-mounted wings. Four fins on solid-propellent booster. 20 ft. long. Carried on ship-board launchers, as well as in vehicle-mounted mobile role ashore. Based in Egypt, kept along the Suez Canal.

**' Guild '** (Russia). Surface-to-air, in service since 1960. Four foreplane control surfaces; four wings with trailing-edge control surfaces. Probably dual-thrust solid-propellent. 39 ft. long.

**Harpon** (France). New version of SS.11. See page 102.

**Hot** (France-Germany). One of three new battlefield weapons being developed jointly by Aérospatiale and MBB. Tube-launched, wire-guided anti-tank missile with flip-open fins. Optical–IR guidance as described for Harpon (page 102). Range 2½ miles.

**Indigo** (Italy). Short-range, surface-to-air. Solid-propellent. Command/beam-riding guidance. Four pivoting wings at mid-body. Four tail fins. Length 10 ft. 6 in. Ceiling 20,000 ft. Not yet in production.

**KAM–3D** (Japan). Wire-guided, anti-tank. Very like Cobra. In service.

**' Kangaroo '** (Russia). Air-to-surface, carried by Tu–20 bomber. Resembles full-size unpiloted sweptwing fighter aircraft, 50 ft. long.

**' Kelt '** (Russia). Rocket-propelled version of ' Kennel ', first shown in photographs in September 1968. Large nose fairing replaces original air intake and small radome. Carried underwing by Tu–16.

**'Kipper'** (Russia). Air-to-surface. Resembles Hound Dog, but smaller and less refined. Carried by Tu–16 bomber. Length 31 ft.

**'Kitchen'** (Russia). Air-to-surface. Carried by Tu–22 supersonic bomber. Length 36 ft.

**Kormoran** (W. Germany). Air-to-surface anti-shipping missile, developed by MBB in association with Aérospatiale (Nord). Same guidance system and low-level cruise capability as Exocet. Cylindrical body with swept cruciform wings and tail surfaces. To be carried underwing by F–104G Starfighter. Length 15 ft. 1 in. Weight 1,190 lb.

**Littlejohn (MGR–3)** (U.S.A.). Surface-to-surface unguided artillery rocket. Optional nuclear warhead. Length 41 ft. 5 in. Range over 10 miles. Ramp-launched. In large-scale service.

**Maverick (AGM–65A)** (U.S.A.). Air-to-surface tactical missile with TV guidance system, under development to arm F–4 and A–7 aircraft. Cylindrical body with long-chord cruciform delta wings, tail control surfaces and Thiokol solid-propellent rocket motor. Self-homing when locked on to target.

**Milan** (France-Germany). Small brother of Hot for infantry use. Range 1¼ miles.

**Mosquito** (Switzerland). Wire-guided anti-tank. Resembles Cobra. Many built in Switzerland and Italy.

**MSBS** (France). Polaris type submarine-launched strategic missile with nuclear warhead. Cylindrical with conical nose-cone, and two-stage solid-propellent motors. Length 34 ft. 1½ in. Weight 39,683 lb. In production.

**Nettuno** (Italy). Ship-launched surface-to-surface counterpart of Indigo. Length 12 ft. 3 in. Range 6 miles. Carried in five-round launcher on fast patrol-boat 'Saetta'.

**Nike-Ajax (MIM–3A)** (U.S.A.). America's first anti-aircraft missile, still used by some NATO countries in mobile role. Two-stage solid/liquid rocket. Radar command guidance. Length 34 ft. Range 25 miles.

**Penguin** (Norway). Surface-to-surface and air-to-surface missile developed by Kongsberg Vaapenfabrikk. In production. No details available.

**Pluton** (France). Tactical nuclear missile developed by Aérospatiale (Nord). Cylindrical body, ogival nose-cone, tail control surfaces and dual-thrust solid-propellent motor. Launched from tracked transporter. First successful firing trials in 1969. Length 24 ft. 10¾ in. Range 6–75 miles.

**Poseidon (ZUGM–73A)** (U.S.A.). Scaled-up Polaris, 34 ft. long. Diameter 6 ft. 2 in. Under development to re-equip 31 Polaris submarines in early 1970's. Multiple independently-targeted re-entry vehicles. Weight approx. 65,000 lb. Range 2,875 miles.

**Roland** (France-Germany). Low-altitude anti-aircraft missile. Slim pointed body. Four foreplanes; rear-mounted delta wings. Length 7 ft. $10\frac{1}{2}$ in. Guidance as for Harpon (page 102). Under development.

**Saab RB05A** (Sweden). Manually-steered air-to-surface supersonic tactical missile to arm Saab–105 and Saab–37 Viggen. Cylindrical body with ogival nose, long cruciform delta wings, tail control surfaces and liquid-propellent storable motor. Length 11 ft. 7 in. Weight 660 lb.

**Safeguard** (U.S.A.). America's anti-ballistic missile (ABM) defence system using a mixture of Spartan and Sprint missiles primarily to defend Minuteman ICBM sites.

'**Sagger**' (Russia). Wire-guided anti-tank missile, vehicle-mounted. Cylindrical body, conical nose and four short-span wings. Length 2 ft. 6 in. In service.

**SAM–D** (U.S.A.). Mobile surface-to-air system, deployed on twelve vehicles, for battlefield and continental defence against high-performance aircraft and short-range missiles. Each launch vehicle carries six missiles in closed containers. Missile has cylindrical body, cruciform tail control surfaces, solid-propellent motor and nuclear or high-explosive warhead. Guidance is by command, with semi-active radar homing. Not yet operational.

'**Samlet**' (Russia). This surface-to-surface version of 'Kennel' (page 38) is used by Russia, Poland and Cuba, primarily for coastal defence.

'**Sark**' (Russia). Two-stage solid-propellent submarine-launched missile. Tapered cylindrical body, with blunt conical nose-cone and cluster of seven first-stage nozzles. First seen in 1962. Length 48 ft.

'**Sawfly**' (Russia). First seen in 1967, this two-stage solid-propellent missile is thought to be a research version of the latest Soviet submarine-launched ballistic missile, with a 2,000-mile range. Length 42 ft.

'**Scrag**' (Russia). Related to the core rocket of the Vostok space launcher, this big three-stage liquid-propellent ICBM has taken part in Moscow parades since 1965 but is not thought to be operational. Length 120 ft.

**'Scrooge'** (Russia). Mobile strategic missile on lines of 'Scamp'. Launched from 62-ft. long cylindrical tube carried on tracked vehicle. First seen 1965. Range 3,500 miles.

**'Scud–A'** (Russia). Resembles 'Sandal', but only 35 ft. long. Carried on tracked launch vehicle. Movable fins for guidance. Range 50 miles. In service many years. Improved 'Scud–B' version on wheeled transporter-launcher, first seen 1965.

**Sea Dart** (G.B.). Ramjet-powered ship-to-air missile, under development for Royal Navy. Cylindrical body, four long-chord wings and tail control surfaces. Tandem solid-propellent booster. Length 14 ft. 3½ in. Semi-active homing. Suitable also for surface-to-surface use.

**Sea Sparrow** (U.S.A.). Ship-to-air version of Sparrow III (see page 98). In service.

**Sea Wolf** (G.B.). Under development since 1967, by BAC, to supersede Seacat on ships of the Royal Navy, for all-weather defence against supersonic anti-ship missiles and aircraft. Also suitable for surface-to-surface use. No details available.

**'Serb'** (Russia). Polaris-type missile for underwater launching. Probably two-stage solid-propellent. Similar shape and size to Polaris A2, except second stage of smaller diameter than first. Length 33 ft. Max. body diameter 5 ft.

**'Shaddock'** (Russia). Surface-to-surface cruise missile seen only inside launcher-container. Jet or ramjet sustainer. Two solid-propellent under-body boosters. Length 40 ft. Range 230 miles. Equips large number of Russian surface ships and submarines.

**Shrike (AGM–45A)** (U.S.A.). Air-to-surface missile which homes on enemy radar. Resembles Sparrow in layout. Range 10 miles. Operational with U.S.N. and U.S.A.F. Advanced version under development.

**'Skean'** (Russia). Scaled-up development of 'Sandal'. No fins. Liquid-propellent engine. 'Silo' launched. Length 75 ft. Range 2,000 miles.

**Spartan** (U.S.A.). Long-range anti-missile missile, developed from earlier Nike-Zeus. Part of Safeguard defence system, with Sprint. Three-stage solid-propellent missile with nuclear warhead. In production.

**Sprint** (U.S.A.). Short-range anti-missile missile. Part of Safeguard system. Conical shape. Two-stage solid-propellent. 'Silo' launched. Length 27 ft. Weight 7,500 lb. In production.